MOUNTAIN
AND
MOORLAND

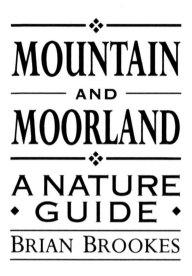

MOUNTAIN
AND
MOORLAND

A NATURE
◆ GUIDE ◆

BRIAN BROOKES

The Crowood Press

Brian Brookes is well-known for his courses on
the wildlife and natural history of the
Highlands. After teaching at Forest Hill School
and the Sloane School, London, where he was
Head of Biology, he joined the Field Studies
Council in Devon in 1965. Until recently he
was warden of Kindrogan Field Centre in
Perthshire.

First published in 1985 by
The Crowood Press
Ramsbury, Marlborough,
Wiltshire SN8 2HE

Reprinted in paperback 1989

British Library Cataloguing in Publication Data

Brookes, Brian
        (British Naturalists' Association guide to mountain
        and moorland). Mountain and moorland
        1. Great Britain. Heathland and upland regions.
        Organisms
        I. (British Naturalists' Association guide to
        mountain and moorland) II. Title III. British
        Naturalists' Association
        574.941

        ISBN 1-85223-225-0

Design by Vic Giolitto

Typeset by Quadraset Limited, Midsomer Norton,
Bath, Avon
Printed in Spain by Graficromo s.a., Cordoba

Contents

FOREWORD

Since 1905 the British Naturalists' Association has provided opportunities for beginners and more advanced students of natural history to rub shoulders with experts, both amateur and professional.

Throughout this time its magazine, *Country-Side*, and its local, regional and national meetings have fostered the collection and sharing of knowledge concerning the rocks, soils, plants and animals which make up our living landscape. Essential in this process of national learning and the spreading of awareness about wildlife has been the publication of many identification keys – keys to groups like lichens, plant galls, harvestmen and spiders, which though present and often abundant in most habitats were at one time frequently overlooked or wrongly ignored, because there was no way in, no key to unlock the doors of enquiry. In the same way, the Association's pamphlets entitled 'Let's begin the study of . . .' helped pioneer many branches of field science.

At last, some of that knowledge, the fruit of all those eighty years of unique experience, is now made public in this superb series of books. Habitat by habitat, all is revealed.

Most of my own knowledge of plants and animals was gained in the field by walking with and listening to the 'ologists', the experts in each subject – bryology, ornithology, algology etc, etc. Each trip was an occasion to be remembered thanks to the personal anecdotes and sheer enthusiasm of people who had all the facts at their fingertips and who loved the subject of their expertise.

If you can't go on such trips, these books are the next best thing. Open up the pages and you can almost smell the sweet or rotten smell of a river, see the rooks flying from the beech hangers, and hear the warm buzz of summer insects or the crisp crackle of a winter morning.

If I may be allowed one personal reminiscence. I can remember following John Clegg (the author of the volume on ponds and streams in this series) down to the ponds in the grounds of Haslemere Educational Museum, where he was then curator. *Stratiotes aloides* (water soldier), *Nepa cinerea* (the water scorpion), *Hydrocharis morsus ranae* (frogbit), *Gunnera manicata* (the giant prickly rhubarb from South America). . . . This was the first time I was ever shown these things and I will never forget either the experience or the names.

I am grateful to John Clegg and all the others who led me along the many paths of natural history and to a very full and worthwhile life. I am grateful too to all the officers and members of the British Naturalists' Association, both past and present, for everything they have done and are doing to share their knowledge and wonder of life.

What a super series of books! The only problem is what is the B.N.A. going to do to celebrate its centenary?

David Bellamy

*President of the Youth Section of
the British Naturalists' Association*
Bedburn, County Durham

 **British Naturalists' Association**

The British Naturalists' Association has existed since 1905, when E. Kay Robinson founded the B.N.A.'s journal *Country-Side* and groups of readers began to hold meetings which gave amateur naturalists an opportunity to meet experts and to discuss topics of mutual interest with them. It is this network of branches all over Britain that forms the basis of the B.N.A. New members are always welcome and enquiries regarding membership should be addressed to Mrs June Pearton, 48 Russell Way, Higham Ferrers, Northamptonshire NN9 8EJ.

During its eighty years of existence many distinguished naturalists and public figures have been associated with the B.N.A. At present the President is Lord Skelmersdale, the President of the Youth Section is David Bellamy, and R.S.R. Fitter, Eric Hosking, Alfred Leutscher, Professor Kenneth Mellanby, Angela Rippon, Sir Peter Scott, Professor Sir Richard Southwood, Sir George Taylor and H.J. Wain are Vice-Presidents of the Association.

Country-Side appears four times a year and publishes articles about every aspect of natural history. Contributions, including photographs and drawings, should be addressed to Ron Freethy, The Editor, *Country-Side*, Thorneyholme Hall, Roughlee, Nr Burnley, Lancashire BB12 9LH.

Introduction

The vast majority of us live in towns and cities. For most of our life our environment is bricks, concrete and tarmac. We travel between home and work in factory or office by car, bus or underground. Some of us would hardly know if it was raining if we didn't have to brave the elements for a few yards between the home and car or between the car park and the office. Indeed, there are city dwellers whose feet hardly ever contact real soil, or never do so. To many people the countryside is an alien world, barely understood and only learned about through radio or television. Yet near to our major towns and cities this countryside is green, mellow and productive, with fields full of cows, gently meandering streams and clumps of shapely trees.

If this soft, pleasant lowland countryside is so strange, how much more strange and remote must the far away hills and mountains seem. Even country dwellers prefer an environment friendlier than the windswept moors to live and work in, and relatively few of us choose to live in the hills of central Wales or in remote Highland glens and to experience the doubtful pleasures of coping with cold, wind and rain miles from anywhere in the depth of winter.

Yet there is great beauty in our uplands and for many there is a great fascination in the austere harshness of solid rock, wild, open moors and the dramatic and challenging landscape. To learn to love and understand these wild places brings a sense of excitement and of contentment. They are special places with long histories, traditions and mysteries.

Broadly speaking, mountains and moorlands, or uplands, can be defined as land above the normal limit for agricultural enclosure and cultivation. A glance at the atlas shows that in Great Britain they lie north and west of a line from Humberside to Devon. Here the rocks are older than they are to the south and east. The moors of south-west England are formed from great masses of granite and the Scottish Highlands from ancient metamorphic rocks, in contrast to the much younger rocks, such as chalk, to the south-east. The oldest of all rocks in Britain are to be found in the far north-west of Scotland, in the pre-Cambrian sandstones and gneiss.

The uplands are sparsely populated, not so much for geological reasons but because it is difficult to make a living from them. The possible forms of land use are very restricted and none of them provide many jobs. The difficulty in wresting a living from the hills results from the climatic conditions at these levels where the weather is so often cold, wet and windy.

Exmoor, Dartmoor and Bodmin Moor are the southernmost of our uplands, rising as islands of granite from the fertile lowlands around them. The contrast is stark when on a winter's day the weather is mild in south Devon, while on the horizon to the north snow lies on Dartmoor.

Shales and slates create the steep slopes, jagged peaks and ridges of much of Snowdonia and the moors and hills of central Wales. Parts of the mountains of North Wales are inundated with tourists and visitors seeking recreation, and there are numerous outdoor centres in the region catering for those who want to walk and climb in the hills. The upland area under most pressure from sheer numbers of visitors is probably not

Wales, but the Peak District. Indeed, for a large number of people 'moorland' is the landscape of the southern Pennines and their notion of mountains may well be the hills of northern England and the Lake District, another popular holiday area visited by many people every year, some touring and sightseeing, others taking part in the many recreational opportunities including water sports.

Near the Scottish border visitors on the hills are fewer. The landscape is less dramatic, without spectacular mountain peaks, but it is no less impressive, with the vast stretches of open hillside and the sweep of the rounded hills of the southern uplands of Scotland.

Once through Scotland's central belt and across the Boundary Fault, which runs from Stonehaven to the Firth of Clyde, one is in the wildest and most extensive area of our upland country, the Highlands. While many parts of the Highlands have become focal points for tourism and recreation, there remain huge areas where a tourist is never seen and stretches of the western Highlands could still be described as wilderness.

In the pages that follow we shall look more closely at the different kinds of terrain which make up the upland countryside of Great Britain. We shall try to understand how the various habitats and communities of plants and animals have formed over the course of time, the changes which have occurred, and the processes which have shaped and are still shaping our mountains and moorlands. We shall take a close look at the most important features of the climate and soils, and at the details of particular plants and animals which

live in these sometimes very inhospitable places. We shall also need to take into account the activities of man — since we and our ancestors have been responsible for creating so much of what we see in our present day landscape and, just as we inherited an upland scene largely shaped by our ancestors, so we ourselves will bequeath to posterity a legacy of uplands which are even more man-made. Year by year we are altering the landscape, sometimes dramatically. Look, for instance, at the extent of afforestation in central Wales and south-west Scotland. A chapter will be devoted to considering upland forests, others to moorlands, mires and mountains. Finally, we shall consider what the future might be, by looking at conservation and the various pressures on our upland environment.

Above all, this book sets out to inform and to interest, in the hope that more people may begin to understand the natural history and ecology of the wildlife of our hills and come to care about its future. At the same time, perhaps those who already know and love the hills will find that a little light has been thrown on some aspect not previously considered, or discover another way of looking at things which will enhance their enjoyment of the upland countryside and make future excursions into the hills even more rewarding. Perhaps also it will encourage those who have never ventured into the hills before to walk over the moors or to go into the mountains, and they too will come to value the wild places and will return to them again and again as places of great beauty and of inspiration to the spirit.

1   MOUNTAINS

The mountainous areas of Britain are situated in the northern and western parts of the British Isles, which mainly consist of comparatively ancient types of rock. The rocks are, of course, literally older than the hills, but the formation of the mountains themselves is the result of more recent geological episodes. Movements of the earth's crust and volcanic activity created our mountains in the first place, then subsequently a great deal of erosion occurred, so what we see today is simply the remaining stumps of much

mightier mountain ranges. Normal weathering of rocks is a continuous and gradual process, but during periods of glaciation erosion is dramatically accelerated. The end of the last ice age in Britain occurred relatively recently and it is estimated that the last remnants of the glaciers disappeared round about 10,000 BC. During the last ice age the moors of south-west England escaped being covered by ice but nevertheless experienced severe climatic conditions. In contrast, the Scottish Highlands were covered with sheets of ice and today one or two places in the Highlands still carry patches of snow which persist for years at a time, melting completely only in exceptional summers.

The movement of sheets of ice and of glaciers across mountains and along valleys was a powerful erosive force, grinding the surface smooth, removing loose material and breaking off protruding spurs and chunks of rock. As a result, today the landscape consists of rounded hills and smooth profiles.

As the ice melted, the material removed was carried away, sometimes over great distances, trapped in the moving mass of ice, until ultimately it was deposited elsewhere. In many cases these glacial deposits were subsequently picked up by rivers, particularly where there was a lot of water from the melting ice, and were washed into valley bottoms or lowlands as fluvio-glacial deposits.

If you examine the material in a deposit you will find there are many different types of rock in it, which is how you can recognise the material as a deposit in the first place. But you can go further than this and establish whether the deposit is glacial or fluvio-glacial in origin by examining the rocks, stones and boulders within it. Material transported by ice in an ice-sheet or glacier is embedded in it and protected by the mass of ice. So when the chunks and fragments of rock are finally released by the melting ice, they are in more or less the same state as when they were originally picked up and the pieces are likely to be angular in shape with sharp edges, just as if they were freshly broken. However, even a short journey in water, with all the pieces of rock constantly moving and colliding with each other, tends to round off the outlines of the rocks and smooth their edges.

The amount of material, and hence the depth of the deposit, varies considerably from place to place – from many metres of fluvio-

Steep cliffs and scree – Corrie Kander, Aberdeenshire.

glacial sand and pebbles in the valleys to just a few centimetres of glacial drift (called 'till') on the hillsides, with here and there the bare bedrock itself fully exposed.

But the process of erosion is continuous and the action of wind, frost and rivers slowly picks out different types of rock and bands of harder or softer material, etching new features on the mountainside. At the foot of a steep cliff you will find chunks of rock fallen from the cliff face, which over a period of time gradually accumulate to form a steep scree slope of loose boulders. Where a small stream wears a channel in the underlying rock a steep-sided gorge is formed and should the stream encounter a less easily eroded band of harder rock, a waterfall occurs.

All our mountain landscapes differ in their constituent rocks and geological history, and in the results of glacial erosion and deposition. So the rounded granite massif of the central Cairngorms is topographically quite different from the serrated ridges of Snowdonia. These differences in geology and topography give rise to a wide range of different soils and drainage conditions, and consequently produce different habitats, vegetation and animal life.

Climate

Perhaps what distinguishes the montane environment from all others most markedly is the climate. If mountains are defined as ground above 600 metres or so, then the climatic conditions are of course severe and will usually limit the kinds of plants and animals that can exist there.

Since mountains have more frequent and more severe frosts than lowland areas, they have a shorter growing season for plants and a prolonged period of lying snow. Conditions also become increasingly wet with increasing altitude, both in terms of higher relative humidity and greater precipitation. The frequency and strength of the winds are important factors too when considering the

impact of the montane climate on wildlife. The sheer mechanical effect of the wind can cause physical damage to vegetation and this factor is more responsible than any other for restricting the growth of trees to the lower slopes. The force of strong winds is probably felt most keenly on the summit plateaux and peaks of the mountains and on the spines of ridges lower down. In such situations vegetation is stunted – quite old plants of heather may be only 2 or 3cm high and prostrate or creeping species have an advantage – and plants like mountain azalea (*Loiseleuria procumbens*) and least willow (*Salix herbacea*) occur very frequently and may even attain dominance.

The former is a miniature azalea-like shrub which grows close to the ground. Its dark green, narrow, glossy leaves are scarcely remarkable and it can easily be mistaken for a dwarf heathery plant unless it is in flower, when the vivid pink flowers, often produced in profusion, make it very conspicuous. Indeed, when the plant is really abundant and is in full flower, the effect can only be likened to a carpet of candy floss.

The least willow must be the mountain shrub *par excellence*. A woody shrub it certainly is, yet this is anything but obvious at first sight because the branches and twigs are all underground. One individual plant, if it is old, may cover an area of several square metres, but there will be nothing to indicate its presence except for the young shoots bearing leaves and flowers during the summer. Like all willows, there are both male and female plants and it is the white, fluffy seeds escaping from the ripe capsules on the female plants in late summer which are conspicuous and draw attention to this remarkable plant.

The effect of wind in the mountain habitat is not always direct or obvious. During the winter a thick blanket of snow provides protection and insulation for living things buried beneath. Where this protective blanket is consistently blown away the vegetation is

exposed to the full severity of the low temperatures; worse still, a strong wind in winter often carries with it millions of small, sharp crystals of ice and in exposed places the vegetation is cut, torn and literally abraded by needle-like ice crystals.

Unlike the exposed summits and ridges, which tend to be blown clear of snow, hollows and sheltered depressions on the hillsides accumulate drifted snow. Although this affords protection to the vegetation beneath, the length of time that different plants are able to tolerate continuous snow cover varies from species to species. There are some plants, mostly mosses and liverworts, specifically adapted to life in such places which can tolerate a long period of snow cover and need only a short snow-free period each year in order to grow and reproduce. The vegetation of these areas is certainly distinctive – in fact it is often referred to as 'snow patch vegetation'.

Common ling heather (*Calluna vulgaris*) is

Alpine clubmoss, a frequent plant of snow hollows.

unable to tolerate more than six months of snow cover and requires the other six months of the year in which to grow and complete its reproductive cycle from flower bud to ripe seeds. In Britain conditions are unsuitable for heather above approximately 900 metres because above that altitude snow quite often lies for more than six months. At and around 900 metres heather is able to grow on hummocks and ridges where the wind reduces the depth of snow and hence the length of time it lies before melting – but it is not able to grow in the hollows, since the snow lingers there. Instead, the hollows contain more snow-tolerant species, such as mat grass (*Nardus stricta*) and bilberry (*Vaccinium myrtillus*).

Further up the mountain the snow lies too

Above Mountain azalea is a low-growing shrub capable of growing in the most exposed sites.

Below *Rhacomitrium* – the dominant moss of high plateaux.

long even for mat grass or bilberry to survive and these are replaced as the dominant species by even more snow-tolerant plants. Above 1,000 metres the vegetation is likely to be mostly mosses, with scattered grasses and sedges. Very often it consists of a close mat of *Rhacomitrium* moss, with scattered tufts of stiff sedge (*Carex bigelowii*) poking out through the moss carpet, and an abundant and varied mixture of lichens.

Light

Light conditions too are an important ecological factor affecting plant life on mountains. The total amount of light over the course of a year increases with altitude, but it is the quality rather than the quantity of light which is more important. In particular, the ultra-violet radiation in sunlight is significantly higher at greater altitudes and higher levels of ultra-violet stunt the growth of plants, producing a dwarfing effect, even on lichens. Another result of the high radiation levels during prolonged periods of sunshine at high altitude is for the internal temperatures inside the leaves of plants to rise considerably. It is interesting to note that very few of our mountain flowers have wide, flat leaves, which would trap a lot of radiation. One that does is cloudberry (*Rubus chamaemorus*), the leaves of which are flat and round, averaging about 5 or 6 centimetres in diameter. The temperature inside the tissue of a cloudberry leaf during a spell of sunshine has been measured as being as high as 40°C – quite hot enough to damage the tissue and to kill some of the living cells. Only plants growing in wet sites seem to be able to survive this sort of experience and it is quite clear that at high altitudes there are no broadleaved species growing on dry sites. The very few broad-leaved species which do exist are restricted to wet places. Even so, after a spell of hot, sunny weather you will find that many of the leaves of cloudberry plants growing at high levels have become blotchy with dead and dying

Cloudberry, showing its broad leaves.

brown patches on them, which is a sign of the leaf tissue having been actually cooked to death by the high temperatures built up inside. Cloudberry is a plant of peaty areas and can occur on lowland raised bogs as well as on upland blanket bogs. It is quite frequent even on fragmentary pieces of peat in mountains in the north of Britain. As the Latin name *Rubus* indicates, it is closely related to brambles, but it is a short creeping plant, producing a few solitary white flowers. The fruit is distinctly blackberry-like in shape and ripens from a bright red colour (when it is very conspicuous, but inedible) to a delicate apricot colour when it is fully ripened and very edible indeed. It fruits commonly in the north but, whether as a result of climatic or genetic changes, does so less frequently in the southern part of its range. In Scandinavia it fruits abundantly and is used extensively in the preparation of pies, jams and liqueurs.

Plants

Overall, the mountain climate tends to be cold, wet and windy, and these conditions make the process of pollination and seed formation difficult. But sometimes even on the very summits the weather is warm, dry and still, so that pollinating insects such as small moths can be seen visiting the flowers collecting nectar and transferring pollen from flower to flower as they go. But such days are rare. Indeed, in some years there is not a single day when such an event can occur. Not surprisingly all our true mountain plants are perennials, so the production of viable seed is not essential every year, as it is with annual species. Furthermore, many of them have developed supplementary methods of reproduction to back up reproduction by seed. These are vegetative methods and usually augment sexual reproduction. In many cases plants have developed a viviparous potential – that is, they can produce small plantlets in their flower heads, where you would

ordinarily expect to find flowers. In some species the viviparous condition is the normal one and flowers are rarely formed. Alpine meadow grass (*Poa alpina*) and viviparous fescue grass (*Festuca vivipara*) invariably have viviparous heads. The exceedingly rare drooping saxifrage (*Saxifraga cernua*) of the Scottish Highlands produces small red bulbils in the axils of its upper leaves, which eventually sprout leaves of their own, become detached and spread the plant vegetatively. This appears to be what normally happens and the one or two white flowers at the top of the stem are often not produced at all.

The climatic conditions which make pollination and seed production difficult become progressively more severe with increasing altitude, so that a climatic gradient exists from lowland conditions at the bottom to severe montane conditions at the top. This gradient is exactly reflected in the condition of viviparous bistort (*Polygonum viviparum*), a small, slender member of the dock family with a simple spike of white flowers. At the bottom of the flower head there are small plantlets instead of normal flowers and the ratio of viviparous plantlets to flowers correlates precisely with altitude, the proportion of bulbils increasing and the proportion of normal flowers decreasing with greater altitude. It has even been suggested that one could use this information to determine altitude when lost in the hills!

Soils

The development of soils on a mountain depends upon many factors, not least the parent rocks which form the raw material. Consequently, there is a variety of different soils on our mountains. In areas of limestone or other calcareous rocks the soils may be basic (alkaline) and support rich and varied communities. More often the parent material is acidic, giving poorer, more acid soils with less variety of species. But, apart from the dif-

Viviparous fescue grass.

limiting factor in soil formation. In the extreme case of a vertical or overhanging cliff face, soil formation may be impossible or else restricted to tiny cracks and crevices. On steep slopes a soil may accumulate, but may well be somewhat unstable. Such soils are likely to 'creep' or slump down the slope, particularly where there is active freezing and thawing going on – which is of course quite a common situation on mountains. As a result the surface of the slope often becomes wrinkled with little steps called terracettes.

The early stages of soil formation from seemingly bare rock surfaces can be seen on cliffs or on the scree of loose material at the base of a cliff. Such rock surfaces are really not bare at all and more often than not the true rock surface is completely hidden by an encrusting growth of lichens, with none of the colour or texture of the actual rock visible.

These lichens are mostly crustose lichens, which grow firmly attached to the rock surface – indeed they penetrate the surface slightly and cannot be peeled off or separated from the underlying rock. A few may be foliose lichens, which grow as a branching ribbon of lichen tissue flat on the rock, without penetrating the surface and can easily be peeled away and detached. Even fewer may be fruticose lichens, which grow upright as little branched bushy-shaped plants from a 'stem'. Very gradually mineral particles are detached from the rock by the climatic action of frost and rain and by the growth of crustose lichens. To these particles dead fragments of lichens add organic matter and the rudimentary beginnings of a soil start to accumulate. After a very long time further accumulation may result in a little pocket of soil sufficient to support small rooted plants and these in turn contribute organic matter to the soil in the shape of dead leaves and roots, so that the soil continues to develop. These slow but quite definite changes in the habitat, from bare rock surface to a well developed soil, are reflected in changes in the plant communities which

ferent rocks involved, the soils on mountains are much influenced by climate and topography. Given the predominantly cool and wet climatic conditions, the rate of organic decomposition in mountain soils is generally slow, so they are often rich in humus or, if wet enough, even develop a layer of peat.

Topography is important in influencing drainage conditions and so affects podsolisation (production of the leached acid soil known as podsol) and peat formation. Also, especially in mountainous country, the slopes may in places be so severe as to become a

Rhizocarpon – a common cosmopolitan lichen which colonises bare rock.

can exist there – from a few highly specialised pioneer lichens to what may be quite a varied little community of different species of plants. This sort of pattern of change, whereby over a period different species come and go as habitat conditions alter, is called succession.

Quite often, as in a case like this, the plants themselves contribute to changes which may lead to their own downfall. Hand in hand with the interrelated changes in soil and vegetation will be a parallel succession of animal species – from mobile, specialised opportunists at the beginning to more competitive, stable species in more complicated communities later in the sequence.

Succession is a universal and common process, but it happens much faster in some places than in others. The rate at which a freshly cultivated patch of garden becomes invaded by weeds and turns into a jungle of nettles or willow herb is much faster than the rate of succession on a tiny ledge high up on a mountain where the rocks and climate are less conducive to change and it may take centuries for a reasonable soil to develop.

Some rocks weather more quickly than others, so the speed at which the soil forms depends upon the type of rock concerned. Generally the metamorphic rocks – which have been subjected to heating and intense pressures – have a layered structure, with the mineral crystals inside them arranged in lines. This usually makes it easier for water to penetrate into the rock, so weathering can be quite quick compared with igneous rocks, for

Opposite Tufted saxifrage – a rare plant of high mountains.

example, which lack this layered arrangement, the constituent crystals being more or less randomly arranged.

The fertility of the resulting soil also depends on the chemical composition of the parent rock. A rock with a lot of calcium in it, such as limestone, produces soil rich in calcium. At the other extreme a rock like quartzite, which consists of a single mineral, quartz, may be chemically fairly pure and contain few nutrients. Indeed, the only elements present in quartzite in its purest form are silicon and oxygen. As a result, although organisms in the resulting soil can acquire hydrogen and nitrogen from water and air, the absence of essential nutrients such as phosphorus and potash offers scant support for any form of life.

Whatever the rock, though, on any mountain the best source of mineral nutrients is to be found where the rock is weathering most quickly. At the base of a cliff or scree a constant supply of fresh nutrients is available

Above Alpine meadow rue is a common plant of calcareous places on mountains.

Yellow mountain saxifrage grows beside
mountain streams.

as a result of the continual weathering of the
exposed rock surfaces and such places quite
often have different vegetation from the
adjacent slopes. For example, while most of
the mountainside may be covered with sheets
of purple heather, just around an outcropping
boulder or cliff there may be a narrow belt of
rich grassland.

These are flushes – places which are rich in
nutrients compared with the surrounding
terrain. They can be either dry, as in the above
example, or wet. The enrichment of wet
flushes results from the local discharge of
nutrients dissolved in water. These may, of
course, be picked up some distance away by
water percolating through surface deposits or
the bedrock itself which reaches the surface as
a spring or seepage line somewhere else. The

plant communities to be found around springs
and in wet flushes are fundamentally quite
different from those on the surrounding hillsides, even where there is little difference in
general wetness. Usually the difference is so
dramatic that one can virtually draw a line on
the ground as the boundary between the two
communities.

In many mountain springs the dominant
plants are bryophytes (mosses and various
leafy liverworts) and there is a distinct group
of plants which occur repeatedly in these situations. The mosses *Philonotis fontana* and
Dicranella palustris, appear always to occur
together and exclusively in these places. They
are both very faithful to this community and
have a high frequency. A flowering plant that
behaves similarly is the starry saxifrage
(*Saxifraga stellaris*), the neat rosettes of which
sit on the bryophyte cushions and produce, on
short upright stems, most attractive white
starry flowers exquisitely patterned with tiny

red and orange dots. Most saxifrages are plants of mountains and at the edge of a spring or over the whole area of a wet flush another species, the yellow mountain saxifrage (*Saxifraga aizoides*), may occur in great quantity, creating a wide border to the stream or a carpet across the flush and forming a blaze of yellow in early summer when it is covered in flowers. Many of the saxifrages are quite rare and in need of protection. One of the scheduled rare species, for instance, is the tufted saxifrage (*Saxifraga cespitosa*), with pale lemon flowers and greyish foliage, which seems to grow straight out of the rock. Its distribution is restricted to a few high mountains in Scotland and one small area in North Wales and it has recently been the subject of detailed research.

Arctic alpines

Habitat conditions on British mountains at about 600–1300 metres are similar in terms of climate and soils to those at much lower altitudes further north. Indeed, plants which only occur high up in the mountains of Wales, northern England or the southern Highlands may be found at sea level in the north of Scotland. Moss campion (*Silene acaulis*) is closely related to the red and white campions of lowland hedgerows and woods, but it is much smaller in all its parts and grows as a short, dense cushion of crowded shoots forming a compact mat on the ground. The cheerful pink flowers are made more conspicuous *en masse* by the contrast between them and the bright red buds. It occurs on open gravelly ground and on cliff ledges high in the mountains of North Wales, yet thrives by the sea in Sutherland. This is simply a reflection of the fact that there is a close similarity between conditions on our mountains and conditions in the Arctic and explains why many of our mountain species are arctic species.

Conversely, further south, in continental Europe, similar habitats occur at much higher

altitudes – at 2,000 metres or so – in places like the Alps. Indeed, many of our mountain species are alpine species and a high proportion of the specialised flora of British mountains consists of arctic-alpine species, which grow both in the Arctic and in the Alps.

There are some exceptions. Another small cushion-forming plant which at first glance may well be mistaken for moss campion without flowers and which occurs in much the same sort of places has small, inconspicuous greenish flowers. This is mossy cyphel (*Cherleria sedoides*), an alpine species which is at its northern limit in Britain and does not occur at all in the Arctic. In contrast, the alpine foxtail grass (*Alopecurus alpinus*), despite its name, is an arctic species at the southern end of its range in Britain.

Just how a plant acquires an arctic-alpine distribution is an interesting question. Is it achieved by seeds being carried from mountain to mountain, sometimes over great distances, even over the sea? Or is the present distribution the remains of a much more widespread pattern dating from just after the last ice age, when these plants were not confined to isolated mountain sites? No doubt both these theories contribute to the explanation. In some cases, it may be that individual plants avoided destruction when here and there, during a glacial period, a mountain peak escaped being covered by the ice sheet which denuded the rest of the country. These 'nunataks' may well have acted as refuges for mountain species, from which they later spread.

Animals

For an animal life in a mountainous habitat is never easy and few species have adapted to the rigorous demands of the mountain environment. For most of them the answer to surviving the worst part of the year, the mountain winter, is to spend it in an inactive or resting state. Most insects overwinter as eggs or as

Moss campion, growing at sea level in the north of Scotland.

pupae safely buried in the soil. Many other animals take the easy option and simply migrate during winter to places where it is easier to live. This may be on a modest local scale as with red deer, which move to lower ground when the weather is bad or the hills are covered with snow, or it may involve greater distances as with dunlin or golden plover, which come to the mountains in spring and summer to breed but move to the coast during the winter.

Few large animals can withstand the severe climatic conditions and find sufficient food to enable them to remain on our mountains throughout the year. The ptarmigan and the blue hare probably come closest to this in Britain. Both are able to dig and scrape for food under the snow, but in bad weather even these hardy specialists are forced to seek refuge on lower ground.

Ptarmigan are close relatives of the red grouse, but inhabit the tops of the hills, running and flying among the boulders of the high plateaux. They rely a good deal on their mottled grey and brownish plumage for camouflage against stony backgrounds, though if sufficiently disturbed they take off, whirring their conspicuous white wings and rattling out their mechanical churring call. Like the red grouse, they will eat most things in the way of tender shoots or plump insects. However, their staple diet seems to be the leaves and shoots of bilberry plants (*Vaccinium myrtillus*) and in the autumn they are especially partial to the berries, which do wonders for the colour of their droppings!

The ptarmigans' response to the approach of winter is to moult into a special all-white winter plumage. Since their legs are covered with feathers, the only non-white parts are the head and feet. Against a background of snow there is no denying they are difficult to see and their winter plumage serves as effective camouflage. However, the change to white in the autumn and back to grey-brown in the spring is controlled by the time of year and not by whether there happens to be any snow or not – so if there is a period of winter without snow or if the snow is late in arriving or early melting, their winter plumage provides no camouflage at all and the all-white ptarmigan stand out like a sore thumb. The main advantage in being white in winter therefore appears to be related to heat conservation in that a white body loses less heat by radiation than a dark one.

The blue hare (*Lepus timidus*) is related to the brown hare of the lowlands, but is smaller and is more closely related to the snowshoe hare of North America. Like the ptarmigan,

the blue hare moults into a white coat for winter. Even the soles of their feet turn white and the only non-white parts of the body are the eyes and the black tips of the ears, which are not easy to see from a distance. This can produce a particularly eerie impression for an observer, when the invisible hares in their winter coats run up a snow-covered slope, leaving a trail of visible footprints behind them.

At the top of the food chain in the mountain community are the largest predatory species and in the mountains of north-west England and in Scotland the very largest

Ravens – birds of cliffs and open country feeding principally on carrion.

A blue hare listens for sounds of danger.

may well be the golden eagle. By far the biggest of the birds of prey in our uplands, the golden eagle feeds principally upon mountain hares and carrion. In practice a high proportion of its diet consists of the carcasses of sheep and deer. All species at the ends of food chains are vulnerable to the toxic effects of poisons which, although present in sub-lethal doses in their prey, may persist and accumulate to harmful levels over a period of time in the predator. At one time the most significant threat of this type to golden eagles was the use of certain organochlorine insecticides in sheep dips, which insidiously built up in the bodies of the eagles as they fed upon the carcasses of sheep that had died from other causes. Now that the problem has been recognised and the chemicals in sheep dips modified the eagle population has recovered, is stable over much of the country and is even extending its range.

Eagles build their eyries on mountain ledges or in trees, often in stunted or bushy trees in rocky gullies, and although each pair only occupies one eyrie each year they may have two or three sites within their territory on which they will rear usually a single eaglet. The size of the territory may be several square miles and most of this needs to be open country such as bare mountain summits and

The dotterel breeds on high ground, but moves to lower areas in winter.

open moorland, in which they can hunt for food, rather than woodland and forest. Because their territories are so big, they are difficult birds to find other than at the eyrie and though many people are convinced they have seen an eagle, very few have actually done so. Often the much smaller and commoner buzzard is mistaken for an eagle, but anyone who has had the good fortune to watch golden eagles gliding effortlessly across a hillside or soaring out of sight on massive, broad wings will never confuse this magnificent bird with anything else.

The largest upland mammal is the largest extant land mammal in Britain, the red deer (*Cervus elephas*). Originally a forest animal, it has increasingly been driven into wilder and more open country as our uplands have become progressively deforested and human pressures on the lower ground have increased. In winter red deer move down from the mountains to the moorland slopes and lower still to farmland, particularly at night or in prolonged spells of bad weather. In summer they move back to higher ground. They live not in family groups as the roe deer, but in herds. The stags usually spend the summer in small herds of perhaps a dozen or so, but in early June the hinds are concerned with

Above Golden eagle – an eaglet at a cliff-top eyrie.

Below Eagles often build their eyries in stunted or bushy trees in rocky gullies.

Above A red deer stag roaring in rut, with a group of hinds.

Below Red deer stag in summer velvet.

calving and come together in large numbers, forming herds of maybe two hundred or more. They give birth to their calves in sheltered mountain valleys and the large herd, consisting of hinds, their calves and often year-old calves too, stays together throughout the summer. They use the same traditional calving areas year after year, though they usually have more than a single site and may move from one to another depending on weather conditions, particularly in response to strong, cold winds. Very hot weather appears to cause deer distress and on low ground they are often tormented by clouds of flies, some of which are potentially harmful, such as the warble fly, whose maggots eat into the living skin and muscle of the animal. In hot weather the deer move higher up the mountainside in an attempt to get away from the flies and take advantage of any late snow patches they can find to cool themselves and to try to shake off the flies. In late summer the large herds begin to break up, and the stags take an increasing interest in the hinds and become increasingly belligerent towards each other as the mating or rutting season approaches. This is in full swing in late September and October, with each stag trying to acquire as large a harem of hinds as possible, and entails each stag defending his own group of hinds from the attentions of other stags, while attempting to add to his own harem by depriving other stags of theirs. The roaring of the rutting stags in a landscape of autumn colours, already touched by ice and frost, the short days and the powdering of snow on the summits all herald the coming of winter to the mountains, at once the most inhospitable and most natural of all habitats in the British Isles.

2 MOORLANDS

The broad, open hillsides of upland Britain, often wide grassy spaces, sometimes mile upon mile of heathery vegetation, are 'moorlands'. These are areas above the normal limit for agricultural cultivation (round about 300 metres above sea level), where the countryside is no longer divided into separate fields as it is at a lower altitude. The boundaries dividing the moors are few and mark the limits of ownership or parish, with only a few others as necessary for managing the grazings. Invariably they are walls or dykes built from the stones lying on the open hillside and it is by no means unusual to find a dyke deliberately sited close to screes and boulder-strewn ground so it is easy to obtain building material, or occasionally aligned so as to make use of extra-large rocks as a base.

The limit of cultivation is generally the head dyke separating the enclosed fields below it from the open moors above. In the north of England and Wales and in the Scottish Highlands wherever the hills rise higher than about 600 metres the upper limit of moorland is exceeded and the more severe climatic condi-

Open moorland, Glendermacken.

Above Grassy moorland on Anglezarke Moor, Lancashire, with heather moor on the better drained, higher ground.

Left Sheep and cattle graze below open moorland near Littledale, Lancashire.

tions, especially exposure to wind and cold, produce true mountain habitats.

The most striking feature of all moorland areas is their openness and wildness. There are few habitations, few roads, few people and above all few trees. Here and there you may come across stunted birches or clumps of willow scrub, but sometimes there is nothing you could call a tree as far as the eye can see. More often there are small groups of trees, in little river gorges, on broken cliffs or clustered round a shepherd's cottage – enough at any rate to indicate that climate and soil will allow trees to grow. But why is there no woodland? What is it that prevents the growth of trees?

The origins of moorland

We know that almost all our moors were once covered in forest, though today the upland landscape is practically treeless. We have ourselves and our ancestors to blame for

Leaves of the downy birch.

the process of deforestation, which started as soon as human settlement began. The natural resources of the forest provided building material and fuel for the first settlers and modern archaeological excavation of their dwellings often reveals the post-holes where building timbers once stood and charcoal in the hearths where fires once burned. These early inhabitants of Britain may also deliberately have cleared extensive areas of trees around their settlements to create fields for simple agriculture. Over a long period one can visualise the impact of man on the forest becoming intensified and extended so that eventually the clearings around villages joined up with each other, creating an open landscape with separated areas of forest.

In the fertile lowlands increasing agricultural pressures continue the deforestation process today even to the elimination of the last vestiges of woodland in the hedgerows. In the uplands agriculture has not been so intensive, but other factors have been responsible for the complete deforestation of moorland almost everywhere in Britain.

Grazing

The most important of these factors was the introduction of huge numbers of sheep which grazed across the large unenclosed areas of the hills. The effect of a grazing animal differs from that of a mowing machine in that certain animals select certain kinds of food in preference to others. But sheep will nibble almost anything. Also, whereas a cow grazes by pulling at its food, mainly using its tongue and leaving relatively long vegetation behind it, a sheep grazes with its front teeth and nibbles very close to the ground. The result is that where grazing pressure from sheep is high the vegetation is very short and plant species unable to survive the frequent close-cropping are eliminated. Most significantly, the seedlings of trees such as birch, oak, rowan or willow are unable to grow into young trees that would eventually take the place of the older trees, as they die and fall to the ground. Effectively, by preventing the regeneration of the trees, sheep-grazing alone can convert an area of woodland into open moorland in a comparatively short time. The average lifespan of a birch tree is about eighty years. So, a birch wood subjected to heavy sheep-grazing for eighty years or so, even intermittently, will be destroyed without a single tree having been cut down. The practice of running large flocks of sheep on all the moorland areas of Britain has therefore not only contributed to the process of deforestation, but has maintained the deforested condition.

Fire

So also has fire. In the past, inevitably, forest fires occurred from time to time as a result of lightning strikes, as they still do today. Even though such fires may only happen at intervals of several hundred years on a particular site, they can devastate vast areas, destroying all the existing trees. However, in the years immediately following a fire there is usually an incredible surge in the production of seedlings of fast-growing trees and shrubs, including birches, rowans and willows, and dense thickets of young trees are formed. After many years, the new seedlings of high forest species such as oak, pine and ash, which are produced in smaller numbers and grow more slowly, ultimately reach maturity and the character of the forest is restored. But if forest fires occur frequently, the woodland may not have a chance to recover before being burned down again and a sequence of frequent fires may even prevent the regeneration of the pioneering species.

Over much of our moorland periodic burning is part of the traditional management of the moor. In many areas the intention is to remove the mass of dead vegetation from previous years and to encourage early growth of the grass to provide the all-important early bite for the hill sheep. After a spell of dry weather, on a fairly breezy day in early spring, the dead grass can be tinder-dry and a fire from a single match can spread rapidly over a large area. Provided the fire passes quickly, the dead vegetation will burn away without heating up the ground and so the roots of the plants are not damaged or killed. The removal of the dead vegetation makes it easier for sheep to get at the new spring growth when it comes. Also, the ashes from the fire help to fertilise the soil by releasing minerals from the dead leaf-litter and returning them to the soil, especially potassium and phosphate, which are often in short supply in moorland soils. Such practices can result in very large areas of

moorland being burned at a time. There is rarely much control over the fire once started and whereas some parts of a moor may be burned almost every year, others escape burning for several years at a time.

In contrast to this somewhat haphazard process, some moorland is managed as grouse moor – principally the heather-covered moors in the eastern Highlands of Scotland, the Pennines and parts of North Wales. A great deal of research has been done on grouse moor management and on the whole biology and ecology of the red grouse, and it has been established that the single most important factor in grouse moor management is a proper burning programme. Indeed, on a given area of moorland the grouse population can be doubled simply by ensuring that there is a carefully controlled programme of moor-burning or muirburn.

If they are not subjected to damage by grazing, trampling or burning, plants of common heather or ling (*Calluna vulgaris*) may live for thirty or forty years. They will start life as seedlings, develop into a dense sward of young plants and eventually become small shrubby bushes. These phases are usually called the pioneer, building and mature phases in the heather's life-cycle. You do not often see really mature heather because it is usually burned or grazed too much, but in those few places where it has escaped damage, given the chance, it will grow into a respectable bush a metre or so high. As they get older still, the heather bushes pass from this mature stage to what is referred to as the senescent phase, when the branches open out and collapse, then lie on the ground and ultimately die.

Young, tender, green shoots of heather are an essential ingredient in the diet of red grouse and successful grouse-moor management must ensure that plenty are available. Heather plants are at their most productive and nutritious when they are young, usually from five to ten years old; so, if they are allowed to age

Above Ling heather in full flower.

Opposite (top) A fragment of relic birchwood, heavily grazed by sheep and not showing any regeneration.

Opposite (bottom) Intensive, regular muirburn produces a patchwork mosaic of different ages of heather moor.

Right Old heather in the senescent phase, some dead.

A red grouse, ever alert, pauses while feeding.

beyond about fifteen years, the production of food for the grouse declines. Not only that, but as the bushes get taller it becomes increasingly difficult for young grouse and chicks to reach the tender shoots at their tips. Usually the keeper allows the heather to reach an age of twelve or fifteen years, then he will burn it. This must be done on a windy day during a spell of dry weather so that the fire passes very rapidly over the ground and the heather roots are not killed, only the shoots being destroyed. If it is done properly, lots of fresh shoots will grow from the original roots and if the muirburn is carried out in the autumn new shoots appear the following spring. More often than not bad weather in the autumn postpones the burning till spring-time and a few months of growth are lost during the summer before the new growth starts. If the fire passes too slowly over the

moor, either because the ground is damp or the wind drops, the temperatures in the upper layers of the soil rise too high, the heather roots are killed, and they never produce any more new growth. It will then be two or three years before new seedlings start to grow and grazing is lost in the meantime.

As well as needing young heather for food, grouse need some older heather for cover. Accordingly, the ideal plan is to burn say one twelfth of the heather each year, so that the moor as a whole carries small areas of heather of all ages, rather than to burn the whole lot every twelve years. Where the soil is good and the heather grows fast, a twelve-year rotation is about right; but on poorer soils where the heather grows more slowly, a rotation of fifteen years is better.

The sustained supply of young heather produced in this way not only benefits the grouse population but will be taken advantage of by other grazing animals too. However, whereas hares and sheep may graze over large areas or entire hillsides, red grouse for much of the year are very territorial birds. This means that a family of grouse – a cock and one or two hens with or without chicks – is confined within a small territory of its own, limited by the territories of the surrounding grouse families. During the autumn and for part of the winter this territorial arrangement breaks down and many birds come together, forming quite large flocks, but most of the time red grouse behave territorially and stay within the one hectare or so which is theirs. The programme of burning needs to take this into account and ideally should ensure that there is a range of ages of heather over the whole moor and in each grouse's territory. In other words, each year's burning programme should be designed to produce many small scattered areas which together amount to one-twelfth of the total area. In practice the ideal size of each patch is about a tenth of a hectare. But even that is not all. A tenth of a hectare burned in the shape of a long narrow ribbon has a lot more edge than a patch of the same area burned as a square. Feeding grouse, especially with chicks, avoid standing in the middle of open spaces and spend their time at the edges, near the cover of older heather, so more food is available to the birds if the patches are long and narrow.

The degree of control required in order to burn long, narrow, scattered strips each a tenth of a hectare in area totalling a twelfth of the moor each year on a twelve-year rotation is an impossible ideal. The terrain always makes things more difficult in practice than they appear in theory, but a skilled keeper will come close to achieving it. Starting a fire is not usually difficult, the skill is in confining and stopping it. By burning into the wind and up to a barrier such as a stream or a patch of snow, an experienced gamekeeper can exercise complete control.

Where management by burning is practised the only plants that exist are those which can survive a fire or which have the ability to spread quickly after a fire and can colonise new areas rapidly. Trees do not really come into either category and, together with the extensive grazing by sheep, fire has played a major part in the deforestation process and in maintaining the open, treeless state of our moorlands.

Before deforestation occurred, if heather was present in the original wood it was just part of the vegetation of the forest floor, together with many other species; but heather needs lots of light, so it was only common where there were gaps in the canopy or where the trees were well spaced out. In such situations, once the trees were removed and plenty of light became available, heather would often take over the dominant role. This is what happened in those parts of the country where today's grouse moors are found. When we look closely at moorland vegetation, what we see is an impoverished woodland flora – that is the plants of the original forest, minus those species which need the presence of trees, those which cannot tolerate sheep-grazing and those which cannot survive burning. Small wonder the list of species is short! A square metre of heather moorland may contain as few as five species of plants, including mosses and lichens, the average being about ten species per square metre, in contrast to about twenty species per square metre in woodland.

I wonder how many of the tourists who enjoy the views of our heather moorland through the windows of their buses and admire the 'bonny purple heather' appreciate the extent to which the landscape is man-made or realise that if it were not for the hand of man they would be travelling through a forest?

The original forest

In the climatic conditions that prevail in Britain today above an altitude of 600 metres or so climatic factors, especially wind and low temperatures, prevent the growth of all but stunted trees, though the treeline is not

Above Wood ants thrive in ancient birch and conifer woods.

Left Wood ants' nest.

Opposite (both) Wistman's Wood, Dartmoor.

Below Slow worms are occasionally found in grassy areas in forests.

sharply defined and one may occasionally find single trees in sheltered spots above the 600 metre level. Similarly, below 600 metres there are places too exposed for trees to grow. Of our native trees, the rowan or mountain ash is the most likely to be found at these high altitudes and one can visualise the natural treeline as being the point where the last few scattered trees persist, there being nothing but bare mountainside above them. Below the treeline conditions become more suitable for tree growth as the altitude decreases. The lower slopes of the hills, the zone presently occupied by moorland, were therefore once open, mixed woodland, with trees such as birch, willows, hazel and holly; and where there was rich, deep soil on the hillside as well as in the valley, larger trees such as oak, elm, ash and in some places pine predominated. The exact composition of the original woodland varied throughout the British Isles, depending to some extent on climatic conditions but mostly on the underlying rocks and soils. It is possible, though, to have a fairly precise picture of what these woods were like and even to be reasonably certain about local details.

Three kinds of evidence provide clues to the vegetation of the past. First, in places which have been subject to less human interference than average we can see that the vegetation is woodland. This only happens in places left alone by successive generations – usually because the area was so steep, stony, wet, small or difficult that it was not worth the bother of attempting to cultivate it or of trying to improve it by drainage or by the application of lime etc., and where the trees have had some protection from grazing animals and fire. In places of this sort, fragments of the original forest have sometimes survived. These relics are few and far between in the British Isles as a whole and are usually well known. Over the extensive tract of Dartmoor, for example, woodlands survive in the river gorges, but otherwise the original

oak forest remains only in three places on the open moor. Probably the most famous of these is Wistman's Wood, which has survived on a steep slope covered by large boulders, known locally as 'clitter'. In Wistman's Wood the young oak trees are protected from grazing animals and fire and are also sheltered from the fierce, cold winds of the open moor. As a result, the seedlings are able to germinate and to grow into small trees before they protrude from the clitter and face the full severity of the climate or are exposed to the teeth of the few sheep that negotiate the boulders and graze in the wood. Therefore the wood is able to regenerate, since the young trees survive to take the place of those that die from old age or disease.

Such a small isolated area of woodland is not, of course, precisely the same now as it was when it was still part of a vast area of forest before the advent of man, nor is it entirely 'natural' in the sense of being totally unaffected by human activity around it. But then 'naturalness' is only a reflection of a comparative lack of human interference. Wherever you look, anywhere in the world, there is usually some sign of man's impact and virtually nothing is 'completely natural', as if man had never evolved. These small remnants of woodland, however, probably retain most of the characteristics of the original forest, are undoubtedly 'more natural' than the rest of the landscape and give us some idea of the general nature of the forest of which they are small surviving relics.

Secondly, occasionally it may happen that the pressures of sheep-grazing or burning, which have contributed to the creation of the moorland, are removed. This may only be temporary. An area of newly planted forestry plantation, for example, is usually fenced to keep out sheep and other grazing animals such as deer, to prevent the young trees from being damaged or destroyed. In these circumstances fire is also excluded and the response of the moorland vegetation during the period when it is freed from burning and grazing, and before the young trees have established themselves and the new forest begins to form, can be quite phenomenal. This poses problems for the forester, who is then compelled to resort to weeding techniques to protect his small trees until they are big enough to hold their own.

The reaction of the vegetation to the lifting of such intensive pressures may sometimes give an indication of what the vegetation was like before the pressures existed, although there is no guarantee of this. What we often see in this sort of situation is the growth of large numbers of self-sown native trees and shrubs such as birches and willows, and one has the impression that if the pressures of man's activities are removed and an area of moorland is simply abandoned it begins to revert to woodland.

Neither the existence of relic patches of ancient forest nor the tendency to revert to woodland are any more than circumstantial evidence suggesting the origins of moorland, but there is one item of hard, factual evidence that is indisputable and enables us to know in considerable detail what the past vegetation was like, namely the past vegetation itself. Over most of the country it died, decomposed and disappeared, but where conditions were suitable the remains of the past vegetation accumulated and have been preserved as peat deposits. It is possible to dig up a lump of peat, pull it apart and see the bits of roots and stems of the plants which formerly grew on that spot. Pieces of wood are commonplace and one can handle and recognise twigs and other remnants of the birch, hazel, or rowan trees which grew there maybe five or six thousand years ago.

An expert can analyse a small sample of peat, sort out the bits and pieces at different levels in the deposit, and work out all the changes in the vegetation of the site during the period when the peat was forming. Not only is the plant material of the site itself

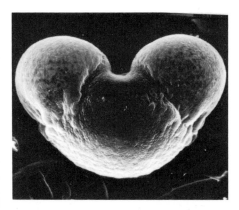

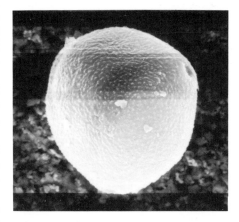

Pollen grains found in peat deposits, greatly magnified: pine (**top**), hazel (**centre**) and willow (**bottom**).

Ancient tree stump exposed by peat erosion.

preserved, but objects arriving from further afield are often incorporated in the peat layer and preserved too. Even the bodies of people buried in peat bogs in Denmark and in England, and their clothing, are found well preserved when excavated.

The toughest and most resistant product of flowering plants is their pollen grains. In the case of wind-pollinated flowers, pollen is produced in large quantities and can be spread over long distances. At certain times of the year the pollen count can be very high, as any hay-fever sufferer knows only too well. Some of this pollen rain inevitably falls in peaty places and eventually becomes semi-fossilised in the peat. As a result, since the pollen grains of different plants differ in shape and markings, information about the vegetation of the surrounding countryside can be built up. All this evidence points to predominantly woodland cover over most of the British Isles in the period before human settlement.

Climate

In different parts of the country different species of trees dominated the natural forest, depending on local climate and soil. This range of types of woodland is reflected today in a corresponding range of moorlands. In general the climate in the eastern parts of the British Isles is continental in character and contrasts with the oceanic climate of the west, where the influence of the Atlantic creates conditions with high rainfall and prolonged periods of humid weather. But the proximity of the Atlantic affects the temperature of the air as well as the amount of rain. The large mass of water in the ocean is slow to change its temperature, so it cools slowly through winter and warms slowly in summer. This effect is passed on to the air masses in contact with the sea, with the result that western areas tend to experience smaller and less rapid changes of temperature, both on a seasonal basis and also between night and day. In eastern areas, further away from the large

water body of the Atlantic, the climate is drier but temperatures fluctuate more, so average summer temperatures are higher and winter temperatures lower than in the west.

The wetness of the oceanic climate results in generally soggy soil conditions, even where the ground slopes steeply. In extremely wet conditions, such as the western Highlands of Scotland and in Ireland, soils may be permanently waterlogged and generally buried under a blanket of peat and covered with bog vegetation. But where the climate is less extreme the layer of peat may be quite thin or may not have developed at all, especially where the soil is richer in minerals than average. Here the vegetation tends to look grassy, though on closer inspection one finds many kinds of plants, including several sorts of sedges and rushes. Moorlands of this type – with grassy vegetation of various kinds on wet mineral soil in a more or less oceanic climate – are typical of the west central Highlands, the English Lake District and parts of the Welsh hills.

In contrast, on the drier, well drained, sandy soils in the more continental climate away from the west coast the moors are covered with vegetation dominated by heathery shrubs and these are the typical heather moors of the eastern Highlands and the Pennine grouse moors. This may seem a well marked pattern of distribution but, of course, it is impossible to draw a clear demarcation line and one nearly always finds something of a mixture. Indeed, a pattern of heathery hummocks and grassy hollows is common, the two kinds of vegetation being repeated as a mosaic across the hillside, corresponding exactly to the pattern of relief and drainage and to two quite different types of soil.

Soils

Under a heathery hummock there will usually be some evidence of layers in the soil showing up as differences in colour. Normally, on the surface there will be a layer of bits and pieces of plant material in various stages of decomposition, from recently dead leaves and shoots which are still identifiable (litter), through intermediate stages to a dark brown or black powdery material which though organic is amorphous (humus). Beneath this organic material is the mineral soil, composed of fragmented rock material probably ranging in size from a few big boulders and stones to lots of gravel and sand and large quantities of finer silt and clay. The mixture of sizes and the kinds of rock represented will depend on the geology of the surrounding countryside and whether it is of glacial origin or otherwise. The range of possibilities is wide, but one example is the common situation where the mineral material is very sandy and consists of a fairly acid mixture of parent rocks. In such a case a number of layers can usually be discerned in a profile of the soil, easy to see if there is a road, track or even a small quarry cut into a hummock.

The top mineral layer will appear grey or white. This may be a distinct layer several centimetres thick or it may merely be that some of the sand grains are white. Beneath this the soil is a rich brown. The difference is caused by the iron compounds, which are brown in colour, being removed from the topmost layer and deposited further down by water moving through the soil. When it rains in these places, providing it rains hard enough to do more than just wet the vegetation, any rainwater reaching the soil surface soaks in through the porous, well drained material and, as it does so, dissolves any soluble matter and takes it down in solution. Easily soluble minerals are washed away completely and quickly finish up in the rivers and eventually in the sea, but minerals which are only slightly soluble, like the brown iron compounds, are moved much more slowly by this leaching process. Nevertheless, when this happens, the top layer gradually loses all soluble compounds, so in the end only the clean white grains of sand are left. For some reason as yet unexplained some of these slightly soluble substances, including some iron compounds, having been leached out of the uppermost layer, are deposited again further down in the soil – hence the rich brown colour beneath the grey. A soil showing this pattern is known as a podsol and the podsolisation process is easily detected by the presence of even just a few white grains of sand at the surface. There are many variations on the basic pattern. In some podsols the precipitation of iron in the middle layers takes the form of a layer only a few millimetres thick, where the iron compounds are so concentrated that it forms an iron pan, a barrier impenetrable to plant roots and impervious to water, which changes the entire character of the soil. In many cases some humus is leached from the organic material on the surface and deposited as a narrow chocolate-brown layer just above the iron-rich horizon. Such a soil is called a humus-iron podsol.

The heather moorland grows on the podsolic soils of the well drained hummocks. But the grasses, sedges and rushes in the hollows are in the opposite situation, being badly drained and receiving extra water from the surrounding hummocks. This results in more or less waterlogged soils, in which all the spaces are full of water instead of air. Such biological activity by soil microbes as does occur in these conditions has to make do without atmospheric oxygen and eventually the materials in the soil become chemically reduced – the opposite of conditions in a well aerated, porous soil, where they are all oxidised. Whereas oxidised iron compounds are brown, the reduced iron compounds in these waterlogged anaerobic soils are greenish and the cold-looking greenish-grey colour is the distinctive characteristic of such wet soils, which are called gleys.

Heathery hummocks and grassy hollows.

3 MOORLAND WILDLIFE

Moorland plants

Some of our moorland plants are both common and widespread. Indeed, they can be found in any moorland vegetation and are what are known as 'constant species'. Heather, for example, exists in virtually all areas of moorland and so is regarded as a constant moorland species, even though there may be only a few patches of it in some places, whilst it is the dominant species in others. It is of course true that heather can be found in places other than moorland, such as open woods and lowland heaths, so it is not faithful to moorland exclusively. Anybody who tries to describe vegetation and to classify it into different categories – whether different kinds of woodland, wetlands, moorlands or anything else – soon comes up against these three ideas of constancy, dominance and fidelity and has to decide which to use in order to define each kind of vegetation. Constancy is simply an indication of how frequently a species is present; dominance is a measure of the quantity of a species compared to others; and fidelity indicates whether a species is confined to one kind of habitat or is not very fussy and grows in other places as well. A species which is one hundred per cent faithful, which can only live in certain restricted conditions and is only found in one particular kind of habitat is called a 'character species'.

Tormentil (*Potentilla erecta*) and Heath Bedstraw (*Galium saxatile*) are constant species that are never dominant but show a fairly high degree of fidelity to moorland. The bright yellow flowers of tormentil are conspicuous in most places on the moors in summer, from open patches among deep heather to the edges of tracks and among grasses and rushes in wet

areas. A small member of the rose family, it is closely related to cinquefoil – but whereas the standard number of floral parts both for members of the rose family and for cinquefoils (as the name implies) is five, tormentil is exceptional in having only four petals. Its leaves are deeply divided into three to five narrow segments, which are a glossy, dark green in summer, turning orange in autumn. It is equally at home as a short compact plant beside a gravelly track or as a tall, straggling

Lousewort – a plant commonly found in damp or wet moorland.

stem, reaching up to the light through the woody twigs of old heather.

Its partner in moorland vegetation, the heath bedstraw, belongs to a family of flowering plants that is much smaller, but highly distinctive. Their most obvious feature is the way the leaves are arranged on the stem in whorls – so you see a circle of simple leaves, with flower buds or sideshoots in their axils, then a length of bare stem, then another circle of leaves, and so on. The heath bedstraw is a fairly small species and the number of leaves varies from four or five in young plants to eight or ten in fully grown ones. The flowers are pinkish in bud but white when open, and although they are individually very small they are conspicuous as a group. It does not have the ability to scramble up through tall vegetation to the same extent as the tormentil and is much more common in short grass than in heather.

Grasses, sedges and rushes

Grasses, sedges and rushes are always confusing to identify and unless they are in flower it can be difficult to tell one from another. The structure of grass leaves is distinctive, in that they consist of two portions, the lower part being a longish sheath wrapped round the stem and the upper part the leaf blade. This is not so with rushes or sedges, but whereas sedges have a more or less triangular stem, rush stems are rounded. (A useful mnemonic is 'Rushes are round, sedges have edges'.)

Their flowers are quite distinct. In the rush family the flowers have all the usual parts, even though they may be small and inconspicuous. Grass flowers don't have sepals and petals, but are protected by a few greenish scales and are very small and packed together into some sort of flower head or inflorescence. In sedges the flowers also lack sepals and petals and are either male or female. Large numbers are arranged in spikes at the top of the flowering stalk.

One of the commonest moorland grasses

and one which is quite dominant in the wetter areas, particularly where there has been some disturbance of the soil surface or where there is heavy grazing, is mat grass (*Nardus stricta*). This is a poor forage species and since it usually grows in soil lacking in nutrients, it is not surprising that it is of little food value itself. It is very slow growing and forms tough, stiff, wiry tussocks which persist for many years. Where there is winter grazing sheep will begin to eat it and its spread may be kept in check; but where there is summer grazing, sheep prefer the more palatable grasses which are available then, with the result that the mat grass has an advantage over the other species and may be able to spread at their expense, thereby reducing the grazing value of the vegetation. When in flower it is peculiar in that the small spikelets of flowers all develop on the same side of the flowering stem and fit closely against it. When the flowers open and the purple anthers are pushed out to discharge their pollen, it is not an unattractive plant.

The high constancy of mat grass in wet moorland is shared by one member of the rush family, the heath rush (*Juncus squarrosus*), which may take over as the dominant species in some places. The leaves grow from a basal rosette at ground level. Whereas the leaves of the mat grass have their edges rolled inwards, giving them a very narrow and wiry appearance and making it possible to roll a leaf between one's fingers, the leaves of the heath rush have only slightly raised edges, so that they are V-shaped in section and cannot be rolled between the fingers. They are also much thicker and are a darker green. The appearance of the plant as a flat rosette is due to the strange way in which the young leaves at first grow straight up out of the middle of the plant, then bend backwards to finish up horizontal on the ground. Presumably this is a good way of eliminating some of the competitors, though when heath rush is so dominant that the plants are touching each other the

Opposite (top) Tormentil – one of our
commonest moorland plants.

Above Heath bedstraw – a small, rather
inconspicuous plant characteristic of moorland
habitats.

Opposite (bottom) A tussock of wiry mat grass
which has gone to seed, showing clearly the
one-sided flowering spikes.

result of them all trying to flatten out at the same time is somewhat chaotic. Its brown flowers are on branches at the top of the flowering stem.

Soft rush (*Juncus effusus*) is a bigger species and grows in large clumps, often where disturbance of the habitat has mixed the mineral soil with the peaty surface layers. A drainage ditch, even though completely overgrown and non-functional, will generally be marked by a line of tussocks of soft rush. The brownish flowers are arranged in a single bunch on the side of the stem a few centimetres below its tip. Both the flower stem and the very similar leaves are round and hollow, the space being filled with a soft, continuous, white pith. With a little practice it is possible to strip this out of the leaves, so as to produce an unbroken length of pith. When dried this can be used as a wick in a saucer of oil or fat, though a single piece in a dish of cod liver oil does not produce a particularly bright light!

One member of the sedge family, the pill sedge (*Carex pilulifera*), is a character species of moorland. It grows in no other sort of habitat and has a high fidelity. A few centimetres high, with fairly narrow leaves, it is a typical sedge with the leaves arising from a short triangular stem and therefore, when viewed from above, appearing to point in three directions. The flowering stem is about 15 centimetres high and has a spike of male flowers at the top, with one or two short spikes of female flowers just below it. All of which is unexceptional, but after it has flowered and set seed the flowering stalk bends into an arch and rests the flower head on the ground in a very characteristic way. With a magnifier one can see that the tiny fruits are covered with short hairs, and that too is unusual in sedges.

Woody shrubs

In the drier moorland various kinds of dwarf woody shrubs are the dominant species. Ordinary heather or ling (*Calluna vulgaris*) is the most frequent, but it is not usually the only heathery species present. Both bell heather (*Erica cinerea*) and cross-leaved heath (*Erica tetralix*) occur frequently with ling. Although they are so similar in general

Opposite Soft rushes beside a moorland pool.

The shoots and flowers of cross-leaved heath **(top)**, bell heather **(centre)** and common heather or ling **(bottom)**.

A forest of grey and red *Cladonia* lichens.

appearance that it comes as no surpise to learn that they are all members of the same family, closer examination reveals quite obvious differences. In ling the leaves are very short and always arise as opposite pairs on the stems. Nevertheless, seen end-on from the tip of a shoot, there appear to be four rows of leaves. The reason for this is that the successive pairs of leaves along the stem are at right angles to the pairs above and below. The leaves themselves do not occur in fours. In cross-leaved heath, on the other hand, the leaves are in fours, are rather long and are held out sideways so they do not touch the leaves above them, as often happens in ling. In addition, the leaves and stems of ling are usually quite smooth, without any glands or hairs, whereas cross-leaved heath is distinctly hairy, particularly the leaves, which gives them a greyish appearance. When they are fully open, the tiny flowers of ling heather, which create the purple moors of late summer, open out to expose their inner parts. In contrast, the flowers of cross-leaved heath are like chinese lanterns and never open flat. This is the case with bell heather too, though the flowers are a deep purple, instead of the pink of cross-leaved heath. But even without flowers the two plants look rather different, since bell heather is not covered with greyish hairs and the leaves are fairly consistently in threes, not fours. Generally bell heather is more common in dry moorland, while cross-

leaved heath is commonest in wetter, boggy places, but it is not difficult to find places where they grow more or less together. It is also fairly common to find cross-leaved heath and bell heather with the 'wrong' number of leaves, often five – just as four-leaved clover does exist.

None of these ericaceous shrubs is at all happy in woodland (unless it is very open) and wherever there is some shading on the moors, perhaps from an occasional tree or bush or among boulders, their place is taken by other dwarf shrubs like bilberry (*Vaccinium myrtillus*) and cowberry (*Vaccinium vitis-idaea*). The former has a long list of regional common names – blaeberry in Scotland, bilberry in northern England, whortleberry in the south and other local names elsewhere. Bilberry has

Cowberry in flower.

green ridges on its stems and its leaves fall off in winter. Cowberry lacks the stem ridges, is evergreen and the leaves have lots of little spots underneath (these are small, clear glands and do not wipe off). Its berries are bright red and of little culinary interest, unlike the attractive blue-black berries of the bilberry, which make delicious pies and jams – provided all the berries are not eaten on the way home, as they usually are.

All these dwarf, shrubby plants create a kind of miniature woodland community with moist, shady conditions beneath them. In grass moorland, too, the smaller plants in the community are sheltered and shaded by the taller ones. By parting the bigger plants and peering in to the world beneath, one finds whole new subcommunities in their own quite different world. Here, with the smaller species of flowering plants, are the lichens, mosses and liverworts.

Lichens

In dry, heathery moorland in particular, lichens are abundant on the acid humus. Lichens are at once among the simplest of plants and the most complex. They are simple in that the algae and fungi which constitute them are among the most primitive groups of plants; complex, in that they are the product of two quite separate entities, physically bonded together in a mutually beneficial relationship. The algal component is provided with a suitable environment and stability by the fungal threads and the fungus depends upon the photosynthetic activity of the algal cells as a source of food. Though we have hundreds of different lichens in Britain, not many different species of algae are involved; it is the fungal partner which confers the particular structure, shape and colours to the lichen. Species of *Cladonia* lichens are commonly found in moorland. Some of these are shaped like the familiar pixie-cups of *Cladonia coccifera*; others, like *Cladonia floerkeana*, look like armies of scarlet-tipped matches; while yet others, *Cladonia arbuscula* for instance, are much branched and bushy, like reindeer moss. Where there is old heather, more often than not another lichen, *Hypogymnia physodes*, will grow on the main stems and older twigs. This is a flat, strap-like lichen with narrow, hollow segments regularly divided, black beneath and pale grey above.

Mosses

Down below the taller plants, near the ground, there is a different microclimate. Shaded and protected from the wind, it tends to be more humid and mosses often grow there prolifically. Many of these are of the feathery, much-branched kinds, the most common in moorland being *Pleurozium schreberi*, with a bright red stem, straight leaves and branches which are not themselves always branched again. Given suitable conditions, it carpets the ground and tends to eliminate much of the competition. Another common moss with a similar branching pattern, but green-stemmed and with leaves curved to such an extent that the tips of the shoots appear to have hooks on them, is *Hypnum cupressiforme*. In competition *Pleurozium* can easily swamp *Hypnum*, but *Hypnum* has a means of escape since it can attach itself to the bases of any heathery plants and grows up them using little root-like rhizoids, which *Pleurozium* is unable to do.

In autumn, in moorland as elsewhere, leaf litter accumulates on the ground and the fungi become conspicuous by producing their toadstool fruit-bodies in a variety of colours and forms. One of the most delicate and attractive is the horsehair fungus (*Marasmius androsaceus*), which is found in abundance on small pieces of heather litter.

Insects

Although the generally poor soil conditions and harsh climate mean that moorlands are places where plants grow fairly slowly, making them systems of low productivity in terms of food supply, they do in fact support a large variety of animals and insects. Throughout the winter and early spring the invertebrates are inconspicuous, being in a dormant state as eggs or in hibernation, and since warm weather comes late to the uplands the visible presence of invertebrate activity does not become obvious until well into the summer. Then, with spells of sunny weather, the moors seem alive with vast numbers of spiders and insects of every description. The small blobs of white froth dotted everywhere among the heather are cuckoo-spit, which protects the pale, helpless immature stages of

Above The shoots of *Hypnum cupressiforme*, a common moorland moss.

Below The tall cones of stagshorn clubmoss (*Lycopodium clavatum*), often found in mountain grassland and in moorland.

Above An eggar moth caterpillar rests on a willow bush.

Opposite (top) Emperor moth (female) and cocoon.

Opposite (bottom) Emperor moth caterpillar.

Right Mountain argus, a butterfly of sheltered moorland.

the frog-hoppers, a family of bugs that feed on plants, using their tubular mouth-parts to stab the young shoots and suck out the nutritious sap. The adults are extremely mobile and, when given a judicious poke at the rear, are capable of executing what would be truly prodigious leaps if translated to a human scale – hence the expressive, if indelicate, common name of 'touch bums'.

Many kinds of moths are moorland insects and although superficially a lot of them look rather unexciting grey and brown insects, the caterpillars are often vividly coloured and one or two of them are particularly spectacular. The larvae of the northern eggar moth take two years to reach the stage when they can change into pupae and ultimately emerge as adult moths. The young caterpillars, which feed on moorland grasses, hibernate in the litter and humus at the soil surface and the following summer are already well grown when they begin feeding, so that by the end of their second summer they are magnificent, large, hairy caterpillars, with long, red-brown hairs and patches of black. But they are better to look at than to handle, since the hairs have a protective purpose and can cause unpleasant irritation if they work their way into your skin.

The emperor moth has a similar two-year life cycle and although its caterpillars do not grow as large as those of the northern eggar, they are every bit as attractive and as interesting. They are not at all woolly in appearance, but look rather like a flowering shoot of heather – that is, bright green with pink spots. With such perfect camouflage, it is not surprising that emperor moth chrysalids are seen more often than the caterpillars are. When fully grown, emperor moth caterpillars do not burrow in the soil to pupate, as the caterpillars of most other moths do. Instead, they climb to the upper parts of the heather plants, where they spin a silk cocoon about 3 centimetres long around themselves and then pupate. The structure of the cocoon is most intricate, especially the part at the end where the adult moth will eventually push its way through to the outside world. Shaped like a lobster-pot, but with the parts springy and not joined together at the top, it is in effect a one-way mechanism – preventing the entry of predators but making it easy, when the time comes, for the moth to emerge.

Frog-hoppers, caterpillars and a myriad other herbivorous insects and invertebrates feed on the plant life of the moor, and so are near the bottom of the moorland food chain. Some of the animals in the moorland community are partly or wholly carnivorous, getting their food second hand, so to speak, and consuming the plant-consumers. They form the next step up the food chain, which can be visualised as a plant–herbivore–carnivore or a producer–first consumer–second consumer chain. However, it is not quite as simple as that, since some animals have a mixed diet and others change their diet with age or with season. Nevertheless, the basic idea is still valid and the large population of spiders consume vast quantities of flies, mosquitoes, midges and other insects, as do some of the bigger animals in the community. Red grouse, for instance, have a fairly mixed diet, eating a good deal of heather and a lot of insects too, when they can get them. In fact, they are particularly fond of daddy-long-legs (crane flies) and have occasionally been found to have nothing else in their crops.

Birds

Whereas the red grouse's mixed diet contributes to its ability to survive on the moors throughout the year, many birds are summer visitors to the uplands. The curlew, for example, which has an exclusively animal diet, spends the winter on the coasts and estuaries, where it can find small animals to eat at a time when the hills are snow-covered or frozen and no food can be found. Of all bird sounds, the distinctive cry of the curlew

A curlew returns to its nest among the
moorland grasses.

is the most evocative of wild, open places. To
people who dwell on the moors and in the
hills it is the joyful sound of spring, the first
sign that winter, or the worst of it at least, is
over. Later the loud bubbling call, as the bird
slowly floats in to land in its territory,
indicates that nesting is under way and that
somewhere in a clump of grass or rushes is a
clutch of big, pointed eggs covered with
brown blotches. At this time of year the air
seems continually to be full of sounds – the
shrill, neurotic piping of the oystercatcher,
the plaintive 'pee-wit' of the lapwing and
hours of song from skylarks and meadow
pipits. The meadow pipit is the commonest
moorland bird. It is also a favourite victim of
the cuckoo, whose own repetitive song adds

to the general summer chorus.

Meadow pipits, and especially their young,
are also victims of birds of prey. Together
with the other small birds in moorland, such
as skylarks and twite, they are the staple diet
of merlins.

The merlin is a small species, just under
kestrel size, and unfortunately is still an
uncommon bird. Its habitat is wild, open
moorland, where it nests on the ground,
usually in old heather, preferably well away
from disturbance. A favourite site is among
rocks and heather on the drier parts of small
islands in upland lakes. The merlin's hunting
technique is simple, swift and direct. Relying
on speed it flies just above the vegetation and
strikes directly at its victim fluttering about
the heathery tops.

The peregrine hunts over moorland too,
though it usually has its eyrie in the higher
hills. Rather like the eagle, it nests on cliff

Right Lapwings nest in moorland in the early summer.

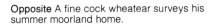

Opposite A fine cock wheatear surveys his summer moorland home.

Below A hen merlin by her nest in the heather.

A peregrine falcon with its young at the nest.

ledges, in traditional sites. This makes peregrines extremely vulnerable to disturbance and interference, particularly as they advertise their presence so conspicuously that nobody could possibly be unaware of them. Any intruder, not necessarily very close to the nest, will cause the adult birds to fly out from the nest site calling loudly whilst circling overhead. In common with golden eagles, the population of peregrines suffered a sharp decline as a result of the accumulation of toxic insecticides in their bodies. Although these chemicals did have some direct effects on the birds themselves, the most serious effect was an insidious reduction in the fertility of their eggs and a thinning and increasing fragility of the shells. This resulted in many eggs not hatching or being broken and the population of peregrines plummetted. Fortunately, there has been a good recovery in numbers in recent years now that this particular problem of pesticide pollution has receded. There is, however, a new and increasing threat from the theft of young from the nest for falconry. Despite severe legal sanctions and active protection measures, it is still the case that many nests are robbed every year. The peregrine's hunting technique is spectacular. It will sit for ages on a rock or tree at a vantage point, appearing completely unconcerned and preening from time to time. Then, as a flock of pigeons passes, the peregrine quietly sails into the air above them and suddenly drops like a stone through the flock of birds, striking one with its talons and taking it with it as it goes. The unfortunate prey is often decapitated by the force of the impact and a few feathers fly, but the most spectacular feature of this mode of attack is the loud noise of the rush of wind as the peregrine pulls out of its dive and goes off to devour its meal or to feed its young at the eyrie.

Mammals

Less apparent are the moorland mammals, which certainly do not advertise their presence in the same way as the birds, though there are usually plenty of signs that they are or have been about. These may be signs of feeding, such as nibbled shoots or the stripped bark of a willow bush. There may also be droppings, footprints or other signs, such as trampled vegetation, and there may even be remains of the animals themselves, such as tufts moulted from an animal's coat, antlers cast by deer or the bones of animals that have died.

Red deer move through moorland on a seasonal basis. They spend much of their time in summer higher in the hills, while in winter they go onto ground below the moors. Roe deer, on the other hand, sometimes occupy open stretches of moorland more or less permanently, although they are principally a woodland species. Hill foxes are fairly common in some places, with their dens usually among boulders and scree, and in some parts of the country they share their position near the top of the food chain with other large carnivores. In the Scottish Highlands the wild cat shares the fox's habitat, making its den among tumbled rocks, and in many areas the population of wild cats is not much smaller than that of foxes. These are true wild cats (*Felis sylvestris grampiae*), not domestic cats gone wild. At first glance they look rather like an ordinary tabby cat, a bit on the heavy side perhaps, but given a good sighting the differences are clear. The wild cat's wide, flat head, with ears pointing more sideways, its much greater size and weight, its shorter, thicker legs, its straight wide back and particularly its short, thick, blunt-ended tail marked with dark rings, all distinguish the true wild cat from feral cats. It has a preference for wooded areas rather than open moors, indeed moorland recently planted with small trees is an ideal habitat. Because wild cats are elusive and shy, sightings are infrequent, whereas the sight of a fox trotting over the hillside in broad daylight occurs much more frequently and conveys a false impression of the relative population sizes. Footprints, easiest to spot after a fresh snowfall, give a more accurate picture of the number of animals about, including mammals smaller than these.

Not surprisingly, fewer small mammals live in the open stretches of moorland countryside than in a lowland landscape of fields, hedges and woods. There are smaller populations of fewer species and the greater the altitude, the more this is so. In grassy moorland the small mammals most likely to be found are voles and in such places the short-tailed or field vole occurs most frequently, although the number of field voles varies enormously from year to year. In most animals there is a fairly stable and finely tuned balance between the amount of food available and the number of animals – with the result that, assuming there are no dramatic changes in other circumstances, the populations remain stable. However, with field voles over a period of a few years the population progressively increases and increases until, in the so-called plague years, the number of individuals is so great that the severe competition for food, coupled with rapid spread of diseases, has a catastrophic effect on numbers.

Wild cats outside their lair in a cairn of stones.

Above Field voles often fall victim to foxes and short-eared owls.

Below Short-eared owls nest on the ground in deep, old heather or long grass.

Most then die and only a few survive till the following spring to breed and begin building up the numbers once more. Predation also increases in plague years and those animals and birds which eat voles, such as foxes and short-eared owls, find a plentiful supply of food.

Short-eared owls look for their food by flying ever so slowly and very low over open moorland. So slowly do they fly, it is almost impossible to understand how they avoid stalling and crashing, as time after time they seem momentarily to stop flying just a metre or so above the ground in order to search for field voles.

Short-eared owls nest on the ground in deep, old heather or long grass. As with other species of owls, incubation begins as soon as the first few eggs in the clutch of a dozen or so are laid – so by the time the last eggs are laid, the first are well on the way to hatching. It is not uncommon to find the last one or two eggs in the nest together with chicks of various ages, while the oldest chicks have already left the nest and are squatting in the cover of the surrounding vegetation. As predators, as one would expect, the number of short-eared owls is related to the number of prey. The unexpected feature is that although the numbers of short-eared owls and field voles follow the same sort of cycle, the peak number of owls occurs before the peak number of voles – just in time to take advantage of the extra food.

4 MIRES

Peat formation

Mires are wet places where dead plant remains have built up to form peat deposits. Acid mires are called bogs; alkaline mires, fens. You can tell when you are standing on a mire because the ground vibrates if you jump on it and if you push a stick into the ground it goes in easily.

When plants grow, whether in grassland, woodland or elsewhere, a certain amount of dead plant material is produced – fallen leaves, twigs, bark and other bits and pieces – which accumulates on the ground as a layer of litter. Some of this is devoured by scavenging animals such as woodlice, mites and worms, but the final stages of decomposition are effected by the masses of bacteria and fungi which abound in litter and the soil and rely upon the litter as a food supply. In this way the complicated chemical materials in the litter are broken down into water, carbon dioxide and simple mineral compounds and become available for recycling in the environment.

Very often the litter rots away fast enough to dispose of all the dead matter produced and, because the speed of decay keeps pace with production, there is no long-term build-up of litter on the ground. But the rate of decomposition depends on three main factors – temperature, acidity and aeration. If the temperature is low, the rate of decay is slow, because the activity of the bacteria and fungi is reduced. Indeed, we make use of this ourselves to prevent food going off by putting it in a refrigerator or freezing it, and from time to time there have been reports from the USSR of mammoths being discovered perfectly preserved in Siberian ice for thousands of years. In some cases we stop food going bad by keeping it in an acid solution, such as vinegar. Pickled onions or herrings do not decompose, since acid conditions make life difficult for certain bacteria and fungi. In nature, wherever the soil and the litter itself are acidic the rate of decomposition is slow; and if it is also a cold place, the rate will be slower still. As a result, in many upland areas the vegetation produces litter faster than it disappears and a layer of dead and partially decomposed material forms on the ground.

Even more important than the effects of temperature and acidity on the rate of decomposition is whether the soil and litter are well aerated or not. Where natural drainage is poor, perhaps in a hollow or where the soil is not very porous, it is generally damp and there may be standing water from time to time or even a permanent pond. In places like this, dead leaves and other plant material often accumulate in a waterlogged condition – and if there is a lack of aeration, or to be more precise a lack of oxygen, this slows the activity of the organisms responsible for decay. The combination of a cool climate and acid, wet conditions generally results in a rate of decay that is not fast enough to keep up with the rate of litter production so that, over a period of time, a layer of dead plant material forms on the surface of the soil or at the bottom of the pond and gradually builds up, becoming thicker and thicker as more dead material is added to it. So long as the litter can remain waterlogged as new material is added, the process continues and creates a layer of peat.

Whether or not the peat remains waterlogged as it grows thicker depends largely on

Opposite (top) The edge of a raised bog, with pools of water in the lagg.

Above Speedwell, horsetail and buttercups in the varied community of a fen.

Opposite (bottom) Looking down on to the surface of a blanket bog.

the shape of the site and the surrounding terrain. A depression on a hillside or in a valley which receives water from the surrounding slopes is much more likely to provide suitable conditions for peat formation and eventually for a thick deposit than a well drained slope or the top of a gravelly hummock. On the other hand, a lot depends on the amount of rainfall. The site will only remain wet if it receives more water than it loses – and water of course evaporates from the soil, particularly in warm, sunny, windy conditions.

Climate

In Great Britain an average annual rainfall of about 1,250mm or more is needed to make conditions wet enough for peat to form on level ground. In parts of Britain where the annual rainfall is lower, the only place where peat can grow is in hollows or depressions kept waterlogged by drainage from the surrounding slopes. In areas with a higher annual rainfall, peat can form on level ground and gentle slopes. And in places where the annual rainfall is far in excess of 1,250mm, it may even be possible for peat to accumulate on fairly steep slopes and for large areas of the landscape to be covered in peat, with only isolated cliffs and rocky outcrops protruding from it.

The result is that on the eastern edge of upland Britain, as well as in the lowlands, peat formation takes the form of isolated fens or raised bogs, while in the much wetter west and north you see extensive blanket bogs stretching for miles. These obliterate any small separate mires that may once have occupied the hollows and depressions, which are now all buried under the peat of the blanket bog.

In the drier climate of eastern Britain and at lower altitudes, where blanket bogs have not developed, it is therefore possible to see each peatland area in isolation and to begin to work out the processes which produced it. Take a small depression in the ground (possibly left behind by the last ice age) with water in the bottom and vegetation growing in it. The water gets there by one of two possible routes. Either it falls straight in as rain or it falls as rain somewhere else and eventually drains into the depression. While direct rainfall is not completely pure, it generally contains only small amounts of dissolved minerals. In places where this is the only source of water conditions rapidly become acidic, since there are no neutralising minerals present. Water which drains in from the surrounding slopes, however, has percolated through the rock particles of the mineral soils and, depending on what rocks are present, has inevitably picked up soluble minerals to a greater or lesser extent. Consequently, in places where there is a source of water from mineral soil, conditions are usually alkaline, neutral or only slightly acidic.

Fens

At the start of the process, the water in our little depression is a mixture of direct rainfall and drainage water, mostly the latter, so conditions are not very acid. But, providing that after decomposition there is a surplus of dead material from the growth of the vegetation, even if it is only a small surplus, the process of peat accumulation begins. Under these not very acid or even alkaline conditions decomposition is easy, so any build-up of peat is slow. At this stage the mire is a fen, that is a peatland system which is alkaline or round about neutral.

Fen vegetation is usually dominated by grasses, sedges and rushes and a rich mixture of herbaceous flowering plants. Marsh thistles (*Cirsium palustre*), ragged robin (*Lychnis flos-cuculi*), kingcups (*Caltha palustris*) and many others make an attractive, colourful mass of flowers in summertime. Under the taller plants the peat surface is wet, with shallow pools of standing water, and is littered with rotting stems and leaves. If the tall vegetation

A fen will survive so long as there is enough water to keep it waterlogged; but, with the peat layer getting thicker all the time, the moment must ultimately arrive when the level of the peat reaches the water surface. At this stage any additional litter which falls onto the surface of the fen does not become water-logged and so just rots away. Indeed, the only circumstance in which peat continues to accumulate is where the vegetation itself maintains waterlogged conditions – and only very specialised plants, namely the sphagnum or bog mosses, can do this.

Bogs

A growing cushion of sphagnum has the ability to hold water, just like a sponge, and can maintain waterlogged conditions well above the free water level. These mosses hold water and prevent it draining away, but – unlike a sponge – they cannot suck up water. So, provided there is sufficient rainfall for them to stay wet enough, they go on grow-ing, producing more peat underneath them-selves in the anaerobic conditions they have created. The important difference between fen peat and the peat formed in this way by sphagnum mosses is that most of the water in a fen drains in from the surrounding soil and so is rich in minerals, but sphagnum mosses, since they grow above the water table, are entirely dependent on rainwater, which has very little mineral content. The peat made in this way is acid peat, so this type of mire is a bog in the scientific sense of the word.

Because bog peat is acid, it grows faster than fen peat – though the average rate of growth may be only two or three centimetres per century and the rate varies considerably from place to place. The growth of bog peat occurs over the whole surface of the mire, but at the edges conditions are affected by the richer water draining down the slope, so the accumulation of peat is slower. Hence the final product is a dome of peat raised in the middle and sloping down at the edges, which

Grass of Parnassus, with its snowy white flowers, is a frequent plant of rich fens.

is fairly open, then mosses and liverworts may find enough light to survive and to spread over the ground. Many of these are delicate, branched, feathery plants which intermingle as a loose carpet. Others are more robust – for example *Climacium*, which with its stout red upright stem and cluster of branches at the top looks like a palm tree in miniature.

The surface of a fen is seething with micro-scopic life and a jam jar of the murky brown water will settle to reveal a fantastic world of flatworms, little snails and insect larvae – a measure of the richness and productivity of fens, resulting from the mineral nutrients brought in from the surrounding slopes.

Above The flowering spike of bog asphodel.

Opposite (top) Long-leaved sundew grows in wet places on bogs.

Opposite (bottom) The insectivorous round-leaved sundew.

is called a raised bog. The slope round the outside is called the 'rand' and the low point between the raised bog and the surrounding terrain is called the 'lagg'. The lagg collects some water from the raised bog and some from the surrounding slopes. As a result the vegetation is usually mixed, forming a mosaic of fen vegetation of various degrees of richness, in which a stream develops and finally carries the water away.

Bog plants

The dominant vegetation on the mire surface is really the ground surface of the bog itself and consists of a mixture of different species of sphagnum in a variety of colours, ranging from bright green and various shades of brown to purple and bright red. Very few flowering plants can live on bogs. Common ling (*Calluna vulgaris*) is usually conspicuous, together with cross-leaved heath (*Erica tetralix*), and from a distance the vegetation may appear similar to heather moorland.

Common cotton grass (*Eriophorum angustifolium*).

Another common species is hare's tail cotton grass (*Eriophorum vaginatum*), which grows as large tussocks. It is one of the earliest plants of the uplands to begin growth in the spring and is an important source of early grazing for sheep. (In fact sheep graze on bogs only in early spring, since at other times there is more food to be had elsewhere.) There is one oval flower-head at the top of each flower-stalk and this develops into the white, fluffy ball of cotton that gives the plant its name. A small

iris-like plant, bog asphodel (*Narthecium ossifragum*), is also common on bogs. The bright yellow flowers are conspicuous in summer and so is the foliage when it turns bright orange in autumn, before it dies down. Another plant frequently found on sphagnum hummocks is round-leaved sundew (*Drosera rotundifolia*), which overcomes the problem of living in a place where there are virtually no nutrients by catching small flying insects on the sticky glandular hairs that cover the upper surface of its leaves. These leaves form a rosette on the sphagnum carpet and their bright red colour, with the glistening of the glands, attracts small flies, whose shrivelled remains testify to the efficiency of this fly-paper technique, which is operational over a period of time, unlike the more sophisticated one-off mechanisms of some other insectivorous plants.

The special plants of raised bogs are, of course, the sphagnum plants themselves, which are able to hold water because of unique and highly specialised adaptations in their structure. The leaves of sphagnum are one cell in thickness, like those of virtually all mosses, but they differ from other mosses in that the leaf cells are of two quite different sorts. Some of them are long and narrow, with living contents including the green chloroplasts for photosynthesis, linked together by their ends to form a branching network. The spaces in the 'net' are filled by much wider cells, with pores in them, and are usually supported by thickened strands of cell wall on the inside. When the leaf is fully grown these large cells are colourless, dead and full of water. Part of the 'sponge' characteristic of sphagnum plants is a result of the water-holding capability of these colourless hyaline cells. This is enhanced by the shape of the leaves, which are rather concave, and the way in which they overlap each other, thus trapping quite a lot of water in the shoot, simply held between the leaves. Some branches on a sphagnum plant grow outwards; but others, at the top of the stem, are short and form a tight head – while other branches, lower down, grow vertically downwards, close to the stem, creating a veritable 'wick' to hold more water still. Finally, the species which seem best at holding water are the ones which have many stems growing close together, forming thick carpets or tight hummocks that can hold yet more water between the adjacent stems.

Walking across a raised bog is not easy, partly because of the softness of the underlying sphagnum surface, but also because, in detail, the surface is far from flat. The surface

Above The heads of deer grass – actually a member of the sedge family.

Left The sticky hairs of sundew leaves trap small insects.

Above *Sphagnum recurvum* grows in the wettest parts of bogs, especially where there has been disturbance.

Below *Sphagnum imbricatum*, a rare hummock-forming species of raised bogs.

of an actively growing raised bog is a mosaic of sphagnum hummocks and hollows. The hollows, which may be an average of a metre or so in diameter, often contain pools of water. These are the areas where you are most likely to discover a sward of bog asphodel or deer grass (*Trichophorum cespitosum*). The bottom of the hollow may be covered with a mat of leafy liverworts or by the species of sphagnum which only grow in water or in very wet places, as a loose carpet or separate stems. These are greenish ones, such as *Sphagnum cuspidatum*. Round the edges of the hollows and pools are those which can hold enough water to grow as a low hummock. These are fairly robust-looking, with very rounded, concave leaves and may be a deep burgundy red, pink, snuff-coloured or olive brown, depending on the species (the snuff-coloured one is *S. papillosum*). The species which can grow highest above the general bog surface are those which form high, tight cushions with tops maybe half a metre or so above the surrounding hollows. Individually these are quite slender plants, but the tight hummocks are a prominent feature. There are several kinds of sphagnum like this and they come in a variety of colours. All of them are green if they are shaded, perhaps by a shoot of heather, but in the open they range from ginger-brown to pink or wine-red flecked with green. The brown one is found in the east of Britain (and in eastern Europe generally), but is rare in the west, and the commonest is the pink sphagnum which used to be called *S. rubellum* but is now known as *S. capillifolium*. It is on these tall hummocks that round-leaved sundew grows, among the heather shoots and cotton grass leaves.

It is always worthwhile to stop and take a close look at plants with a lens. On a raised bog it can be a revelation well worth wet knees. A hummock of sphagnum is a small world of its own. Tiny straggling stems of bright green leafy liverworts find a habitat for themselves between the heads of sphagnum.

Some send out thin white shoots, for all the world like roots, down into the hummock; others produce little upright stems with a pinhead of green powder at the tip, which can blow away and spread the species; and yet others employ the same technique, but produce yellow granules on the edges of their leaves. Under bushy heather, bog mosses are usually unable to grow and the bare acid peat becomes covered with lichens as the heather bushes age and open out. And on the fibrous base of a tussock of cotton grass you may find thin green threads looking like algae but with minute leaves, which are some of the smallest kinds of leafy liverworts. Each is a mini-habitat with its own plants and animals in its own mini-climate. There is even one minute leafy liverwort (*Sphenolobus minutus*) which colonises the droppings of hares; and there are mosses, such as *Splachnum ampullaceum*, that live on sheep dung and bones.

Animals

Both bogs and fens provide a home for some animal life. Look in a sphagnum hummock for small plants and you will often find an ants' nest. Look under heather for lichens and you may discover harvestmen, caterpillars and spiders. What is more, birds of open moorland often nest where there are bogs and fens. Curlew, grouse or lapwings may greet you on a summer visit and redshank often find a good clump of sedges for a nesting site. But the real bogland bird is the snipe. Very rarely indeed will you find the small, round, compact nest of four eggs hidden and camouflaged in the midst of a thick clump of rushes, but the parent bird will often slip off the nest and run unobserved a little way before flushing from under your feet and zigzagging away low over the ground. And for the ultimate in sheer idle enjoyment, try lying in the sun and listening to the display flight of the snipe, on and on, hour after hour, all day and all night – with its rasping, clockwork call as the bird circles high in the air, interspersed with the

Above Very much a peatland bird, the snipe uses its long bill to probe for worms and insects.

Below The redshank is a summer visitor that nests in wet moorland and in fens.

excited warbling, drumming sound made by the vibrating outer tail feathers as it throws itself into long, oblique power dives.

The more remote uplands of the north and west are the territory of the greenshank, a medium-sized wader which is a summer visitor to the hills, where it comes to breed. It is not so much a bird of blanket bogs as of the wettest parts of fens and the shores of lochs. Its nest is on the ground among rushes and sedges, often close against a prominent rock or clump of rushes which will hide it to some extent. The camouflage of the stationary bird is perfect and it is usually only discovered when the adult's nerve breaks and it takes to the air. Its loud ringing cry is unmistakable as it closely circles the intruder, perhaps diverting attention from a family of young ones, and there is generally no doubt of its identity, which is confirmed by the grey upper parts and white underparts of the body and by the fact that in flight the bird trails its feet so they stick out beyond its tail.

Erosion

Not many animals find bog vegetation palatable. Indeed, few eat either sphagnum or

The greenshank nests among sedges and rushes.

The eroded edge of a blanket bog.

mosses in general and cross-leaved heath is a tough, wiry plant with little food value – so, apart from cotton grass in spring, there is not much to attract a grazing animal. Occasionally, attempts are made to improve the grazing value of a bog by draining or burning. Successful drainage can increase the growth of heather and careful burning may cause young heather shoots to grow, with quite dramatic effect since sphagnum mosses are easily killed by fire. But on the whole bogs do not burn easily and the net result of drainage may merely be that the drains fill with water and

become clogged with sphagnum – and so are ineffective, or at best there is a drying effect for a few centimetres either side. Where there has been drainage, burning, grazing, trampling or intensive extraction of peat for fuel or other purposes, or when there has been a local tendency to a drier climate, then the whole raised bog or blanket bog system may change dramatically. Indeed, any of these factors can alter the levels and movement of water and the growth of vegetation in the system to the point where peat no longer forms. In a great many areas, most noticeably near the eastern and southern limits of bog systems, these factors have contributed not so much to the cessation of peat formation as to an actual reversal of the process and degradation of the existing peatland. Anything which damages or destroys the sphagnum carpet on the surface of a bog impairs its ability to hold rainwater and to maintain a waterlogged, anaerobic state. The result is that the surface dries, the peat shrinks and air penetrates the surface layers. This enables decomposition to set in and the peat begins to turn into humus, becoming even more acidic as it does so, sometimes giving pH values as low as $3 \cdot 4$, and the only plants then able to cope are lichens (mainly species of *Cladonia*). Once initiated, the process is self-facilitating and, unless external factors cause the site to become waterlogged again, the mire cannot recover and the process continues until all the peat has gone.

The small cracks and broken areas which appear on the surface at first are eroded by rain washing material away or by wind blowing away the dried up humifying powder, so that channels are formed on the surface which quickly erode further as they become tracks for rainwater and funnels for wind. Extensive areas of blanket bog are eroded in this way, the branching network of channels isolating the remaining blocks of peat, which are called 'hags'. Typically these have some vegetation on top and are undercut by erosion – by the processes of oxidation, rain-washing and wind-blowing, often augmented by sheep rubbing against the hags while sheltering among them. To appreciate the nature and scale of this hagging process and the landscape of degraded blanket bog it produces, I recommend a walk across the southern Pennines or the eastern Highlands. It is not without appeal, but it is an acquired taste.

5 FORESTS

To a large extent the landscape is what we make it and over the centuries the countryside of Britain has been transformed into an agricultural landscape, with the lowlands and most fertile areas cultivated and the uplands and less fertile areas used for animal husbandry. The result is a predominantly deforested landscape, but in recent years efforts have been made to increase the proportion of woodland in our countryside. This has been achieved partly by management of the remaining areas of natural and semi-natural woods, but by far the greatest increase in woodland has consisted of plantations established on previously deforested land.

As long ago as the late eighteenth century enlightened landowners were engaged in the establishment of plantations of trees on their estates and there were important introductions of species to Britain from other parts of the world, such as Douglas fir and Japanese larch. But the major impetus leading to large-scale afforestation came with the establishment of the Forestry Commission in 1919. Since then a great deal of planting has occurred in upland areas, sandwiched between the productive, fertile lowlands, with their high quality soils more suited to agriculture, and the inhospitable mountain environment above, unsuitable for tree growth. Very roughly this is the moorland zone, from approximately 350 to 700 metres. There are, of course, many areas at lower altitudes, where soils are poorer than average, that have been successfully forested, just as there are extensive tracts of open moorland which have not been planted. But most of the additional areas of new plantations in recent years have been in the upland areas of Britain, particularly in Wales and Scotland, especially south-west Scotland.

Although this process has resulted in reforestation, the new kind of forest is quite different from the original woodland and virtually all the afforestation of upland sites has been with coniferous species. The selection of species for planting is a complicated business, but due to the ecological constraints of upland sites and the commercial requirement of rapid growth only about half a dozen species have been involved on any significant scale.

It is a pity that visitors to forests generally know so little about the trees, although they are often well informed about birds and wild flowers. Many a naturalist will dismiss the trees as 'conifers', often with an uncomplimentary adjective, and quite happily decline to discriminate between pine cones and fir cones. Nevertheless, it is worth while taking an interest in these trees – even though, for some, it may only be a case of knowing one's enemy.

Spruces

Spruces are planted in greater numbers than other conifers in these upland forests. Spruce needles occur singly on the shoots and have short, woody stalks. This is best seen by examining the dead twigs at the base of a young tree or on the ground, because when the needles fall the woody stalk remains on the twig as a small peg. The trees have the triangular shape of a traditional Christmas tree – not surprisingly, since traditional Christmas trees are Norway spruce. The other species of spruce which is used in vast numbers in these forests is Sitka spruce, which can easily be

Redpoll – birds such as the redpoll, goldcrest and siskin have increased dramatically in numbers with the development of conifer plantations.

The foliage and cones of Norway spruce (**top left**), silver fir (**top right**), Scots pine (**bottom left**) and European larch (**bottom right**).

distinguished by the texture of the foliage and by the colour of the underside of the needles. A shoot of Norway spruce can comfortably be squeezed with the bare hand and feels rather stiff – but squeezing a shoot of Sitka spruce in the bare hand can be a painful experience, since the needles are sharp enough to draw blood. The colour of a Norway spruce needle is a clear green above and below, while Sitka spruce needles are green above but blue-green beneath. The cones differ too, those of Norway spruce being much longer and fatter than the short, scruffy cones of Sitka spruce. Like all spruce cones, they hang downwards from the branches. Norway spruce is a European species and a constituent of the native

forests of northern Europe. Sitka spruce is a native of the west coast of North America, usually grown from seed collected on Queen Charlotte Island in British Columbia, though Sitka is a small sea port in Alaska. Sitka spruce growing in Britain may occasionally produce sufficient quantities of good seed to form a commercial crop worth collecting in its own right. This happened in 1983 and 1984, when such a bumper crop was produced that spruce seed from Britain was even exported to North America.

Spruces are not happy on dry, sandy soils and are usually planted on wet, mineral or peaty soils on gentle slopes or in lower-lying areas. Sitka spruce has the higher potential

Opposite A plantation of young conifers.

Above Norway spruce plantation in Drummond Hill Forest, East Scotland.

growth rate and productivity of the two species, but it is more susceptible to frost damage, whilst Norway spruce is more frost-resistant. Consequently, Norway spruce is often planted in frost hollows in valleys or at the bottoms of slopes, whereas Sitka spruce is planted higher up, where there is less frost danger and a better chance of the trees, at least when young, being covered by a protective blanket of snow during the coldest parts of the year.

Neither species of spruce has deep roots and both are prone to being blown over by strong winds, so they are not usually planted where winds are likely to be high. Another difficulty in growing spruces on moorland sites is the problem of establishing them where there is heather.

For the establishment of a forest the young trees are raised from seed in a nursery. They spend one year in a seed bed, followed by two years in a nursery bed, and are then planted out in their final positions in the forest. During the first few years the rate of growth is slow. In addition to competition from other vegetation, the young tree has to recover from the disturbance of being transplanted and needs to establish an effective root system. This constitutes the 'lag' phase of its growth, but eventually the growth rate begins to accelerate, the annual increments in size becoming progressively greater and greater, and the tree enters an exponential or 'log' phase of growth. This cannot, of course, go on for ever and eventually growth slows down and the tree enters the final senescent phase of its life. This is the general pattern, but with spruce the lag phase is especially significant. When spruces are planted in heather, as they often are, a situation can arise where the lag phase is extended seemingly indefinitely and the trees are said to be held in check. Exactly how or why this happens is not entirely clear.

Many plants, including most trees and certainly both heather and spruces, need to form a close association in the soil between their own roots and certain kinds of fungi before they are able to grow properly. This arrangement appears to be beneficial both to the fungus and the higher plant – in other words, a symbiosis. This particular form of symbiosis is called a mycorrhizal association. It appears that heather has an inhibitory effect on the nutrition of the young spruce and it seems likely that the presence of heather roots in the soil upsets the mycorrhizal relationship in some way. It may be that the fungus in the heather roots and the fungus in the spruce roots are incompatible. Certainly the effect disappears if the heather is killed off. Nowadays it is common to find this being done by the use of herbicides such as 2,4-D laboriously applied round each individual tree by a squad of men with knapsack-sprayers. In some places the planting of other species, mixed in between the conifers, is effective. Young larch or pine, for instance, are not held in check by the heather and grow away, leaving the little spruces looking stunted. The increased shade they produce soon causes the heather to die, and straight away the spruces take off and quickly overtake the larch or pine, which have accomplished their task of 'nursing' the spruce. The inhibiting effect of the heather can also be overcome by application of certain fertilisers, especially nitrogenous fertiliser, so the mycorrhizal relationship is not the whole story.

Pines

Where the soil is dry, sandy, well drained or acid, spruces can only be grown with difficulty and with the expense of high doses of artificial fertilisers. The tendency is to plant pines in such places instead, in particular Scots pine (*Pinus sylvestris*). These are usually of Continental origin rather than the indigenous British forms, which tend to be rather bushy and branchy and consequently of less value as a timber crop. Unlike spruces, pines have two kinds of shoots. The buds at the tips of the twigs develop in the usual fashion to produce normal 'long shoots'. These in turn have little buds along them which only grow to a millimetre or so in length, forming the appropriately named 'short shoots'. The needles are borne exclusively on the short shoots and, depending on the species, grow in twos, threes or fives. In Scots pine they are in pairs and are typically bluish-green in colour. If the tree is unhappy for some reason, perhaps because of soil conditions or disease, the foliage may look rather yellowish and can be mistaken at first glance for another of the commonly planted pine species, lodgepole pine (*Pinus contorta*). This is a native of North America, from the Rockies, which favours rather wetter conditions than Scots pine and is often planted on peaty soils. It too is a two-needled species, but the needles are always bright green and are longer and more crowded than in Scots pine, giving more of a bottle-brush appearance to the branches. Except during the season of active growth, in late spring and summer, these two species can be distinguished by examining the clusters of buds at the tips of the twigs which will form the 'long' shoots of the following year. These consist of a central bud surrounded by several outer ones. In Scots pine the central bud is only slightly longer than the others, maybe up to half as long again, and is usually slightly sticky with a little resin, whereas in lodgepole pine the central bud is usually much longer than the others, possibly twice as long, and the whole cluster of buds is often thickly coated with a sticky white deposit of resin. When the trees are older they are easier to distinguish. The flaky bark of Scots pine gives the trunk, especially the upper parts, a deep red colour which is absent from lodgepole pine. Their cones are quite distinctive too. Those of Scots pine are rather pointed and knobbly and fall from the tree after three years, whereas the cones of lodgepole pine are prickly and more rounded and stay on the tree for much longer – so, while the cones of a Scots pine are only

to be found on the younger small twigs, those of lodgepole pine can be found on thick branches six years or so old.

Larch

The only other conifers planted extensively in upland forests are larches. These too have a long and short shoot system and after the first year of a branch's growth all the needles are borne on the short shoots. Whereas the needles of pines are in twos, threes or fives, those of larches are in much larger numbers so that each short shoot looks like a miniature shaving brush. At least, this is so in summer, because larches are unique among conifers in

A mature larch plantation in Wentwood Forest, Wales.

Above A toadstool (*Leccinum scabrum*) with birch seedlings in heathery moorland.

Opposite Larvae of the pine sawfly devour all the one-year-old needles.

Left *Coltrichia perennis*, a beautiful fungus frequently found in heather moorland.

being deciduous. In recent plantations the larches you see will probably be Japanese larch (*Larix leptolepis*). The young twigs are conspicuously red, making a fine blaze of colour in the forest in winter. The scales of the ripe cones curve outwards in a very characteristic way that helps distinguish Japanese larch from European larch (*Larix decidua*), which has straight scales and young twigs that are yellowish or straw-coloured. European larch used to be more extensively planted, but although it grows nice and straight it is more susceptible to disease than Japanese larch. On the other hand, Japanese larch has a tendency to corkscrew, especially at the top, when young. The larch to grow, therefore, is the hybrid between the two, which combines straightness with resistance to disease. Unfortunately, however, hybrid larch seed is comparatively expensive.

The choice of site for larch is usually not related to the soil conditions. Often you will find a belt of larches about ten trees wide planted alongside forest roads or around the edges of the forest. It is possible to walk along forest roads flanked by larches and to get the impression that most of the forest is larch, yet not far from the road it gives way to spruce and pine. The reason for this arrangement, whereby a large forest is traversed by belts of larch breaking up the extensive blocks of other species, is that larch does not burn so readily as the other trees and the belts of larch are planted as fire-breaks to control forest fires.

Establishment

The first stage in the conversion of an area of open moorland into forest is to exclude grazing animals and prepare the ground for planting. Sheep are removed and the whole site is usually fenced. Sometimes the fencing needs to be high enough to exclude deer and a great deal of research has been done into different types of fence design. Unfortu-

nately, however, even the most elaborate and expensive fence doesn't work when it is buried in a snow drift.

Preparation of the ground for planting is designed to provide the best possible conditions for the young trees to become established quickly and to begin growing as rapidly as possible, with a short lag phase. Reducing competition from other plants helps and this is often achieved by controlled burning over the whole area. The next stage is to plough shallow furrows, 10cm or so deep, at planting-distance apart, normally about 1·5m. In poorly drained sites or where there is a well developed iron pan in the soil, the ploughing will be deeper to improve drainage or to break up the iron pan so as to enable the tree roots to penetrate more deeply. In the process of ploughing, the turf is turned and laid alongside the furrow and it is into this upside-down turf that the small trees are planted. There they find themselves in a weed-free environment to start with and in a well drained position, with their roots at or close to the compost-like double layer of dead and rotting vegetation sandwiched beneath the upturned turf.

Depending on the precise site and soil conditions there are variations in this general pattern. Sometimes the terrain makes ploughing impossible, sometimes an application of fertiliser has to be given at planting.

In the following years measures may have to be taken to control weed growth if competition affects the small trees. This is achieved by chemical control or occasionally by cutting. The other problems encountered in these early stages tend to be associated with nutritional requirements and physical damage.

It is quite usual for young plantations to suffer from mineral deficiencies, particularly deficiency in phosphate and nitrogen, though the precise nature of the problem will depend upon the composition of the soil in question. If the extent of the forest is large enough to justify it, the appropriate granular fertiliser is applied from the air by helicopter. A common source of damage to young trees is from small mammals, such as voles, and deer. A high vole population often builds up in new plantations, where the general character of the vegetation which develops after burning and ploughing is that of a grassland. In these circumstances many trees may be killed by voles nibbling the bark from them and 'ringing' them at ground level.

Where a new area of planting has been established close to older existing forest the problem of damage by roe deer is most acute and heavy browsing can do irreparable damage to large areas of young trees. If, for whatever reason, substantial gaps occur in the plantation where trees have failed to grow, the forester may try to fill the gaps by replanting or 'beating up'.

Once the plantation becomes successfully established, usually very little needs to be done until decisions have to be made about thinning the crop, when it is about twenty years old. At last, when the forest has reached maturity after fifty or sixty years, depending on the species and the site, and assuming it has escaped all the pests and diseases and has not been blown down by gales or destroyed by fire, then it can be harvested.

The forest community

There is no doubt that forests are among the most diverse ecological systems. They contain a great variety of habitats within their quite complex three-dimensional structure. This diversity of habitat is reflected in the large range of communities and in the generally large number of species of plants and animals that occur in woodlands. There are considerable differences in the conditions and problems of life at different levels within a forest, a phenomenon referred to as stratification, and different species are adapted to exploit each level. For example, birds which pass through the topmost branches, as a small flock of long-tailed tits may do, experience a habitat different from that of a tree-creeper searching the tree trunks themselves for food or a wren that flits in and out of low-growing bushes and shrubs nearer the ground. Generally speaking, British forests may be considered to have four structural layers. The tree layer consists of a canopy of mature trees; the shrub layer, of bushes and small trees; the field layer, of herbaceous plants; and the ground layer, of mosses. Vertical stratification also occurs below ground, since the root systems of the various plants penetrate to different depths in the soil.

Seasonal changes add another dimension to the variety in a wood, particularly where the trees are predominantly deciduous species and so give rise to marked seasonal fluctuations in

Hard fern thrives on acid soils in upland forests and on moorland.

Part of a hillside ploughed and ready for planting.

the amount of shade they produce. The smaller plants on the forest floor react to these cyclical effects and the vegetation presents different aspects at different seasons throughout the year – from pre-vernal (early spring), through vernal (spring), aestival (summer), autumnal and hiemal (winter) aspects and back to pre-vernal. All of these fluctuations in the vegetation are accompanied by corresponding patterns of change in the animal life.

Just as the intricacies of structure and seasonal variation are conducive to a rich variety of wildlife in forests, so too is diversity in the species of the trees. A greater diversity of trees multiplies the available habitats, so mixed woodlands support a more varied wildlife than do forests of a single species. Furthermore, some species of trees make a greater contribution to the variety of wildlife than others. The fact is that over the years a long-established native species, such as oak, acquires a huge number of animal species which depend upon it or are associated with it in some way, be they gall-forming insects or small scavenging creatures living in the litter of dead leaves. On the other hand, trees which are recent introductions to the British Isles from other parts of the world are less likely to have built up relationships with our native animals and so inevitably make a smaller contribution to the faunal diversity of a wood.

In a plantation the fact that the trees are even-aged and uniform in size reduces the diversity of structure at any one time, but introduces a long-term change in habitat conditions as the forest ages. In the early stages of growth, before the trees have grown sufficiently for their canopies to close, there is usually a good variety of habitats with plenty of choice for animals in terms of food supply and cover. The introduction of some coniferous forest into an area which was previously extensive open moorland is clearly an enhancement of the diversity of available habitats and augments the variety of wildlife present in the landscape. Within the planted area the number of species will rise, too. As the young trees grow, however, they become an increasingly dominant influence in the community and gradually the number of moorland species originally present declines and any woodland species present increases. In a conifer plantation at the 'thicket' stage, probably fifteen to twenty years old, when the trees have grown together to such an extent that it is difficult to force a way between them, the densely shaded conditions on the ground may well be such that hardly any green plants, even woodland species of the original birch forest, can survive. Once past this stage, especially if thinning is carried out, a little more light tends to penetrate the canopy and more plants may be able to establish themselves. The shading effect is most pronounced among evergreen species with dense foliage, such as spruces, and much less so under a deciduous species such as larch. In all cases the richest part of the forest will be along rides and around clearings where the 'edge' effect increases the range of habitats once more.

The fall of conifer needles onto the ground tends to accumulate quite rapidly as a fairly thick layer of litter on the forest floor. Usually this will be penetrated by white fungal threads, quite easily seen in a handful of material, which slowly break down the acid, resinous needles to a black humus on the soil surface, producing soil conditions quite different from what was there before.

The relatively varied community of plants and animals in the early years of a young forest changes progressively as the forest ages into what seems to be a very uniform community, with few kinds of plants and animals and a more or less bare forest floor of dead conifer needles. In a long-established forest, in addition to the diversity created by clearings along rides, beside streams and at the woodland edge, the periodic felling of blocks of mature trees and restocking with young ones gradually breaks up the rather uniform age

Green-veined white butterfly – often seen along grassy tracks and rides in upland forests.

structure of the plantation and, although some parts of the forest may be dark and somewhat devoid of variety, other parts will be at the more diverse early stage, so that in the forest as a whole there is a range of habitats and communities, which will eventually become established as a patchwork of age groups with a dynamic pattern of plant and animal distribution. Indeed, the animals and plants which form communities in particular ages of forest will develop in suitable areas and persist for the duration of that stage of the forest's development. Most animals and some plants are sufficiently mobile to get around in this way but some are not and so will be absent altogether.

Forest animals

Several species of animals respond very favourably to afforestation and prominent among them is the roe deer. The smallest of our native deer (though not as small as the introduced and very localised muntjac and Chinese water deer) the roe deer is essentially a forest animal. As with most deer in the wild, it is difficult to find and watch roe deer without

frightening them. On the other hand, evidence of their presence in a wood is normally both abundant and obvious, often including a trail of footprints or 'slots'. In common with other ungulate mammals they have two toes on each foot and the slots of a roe deer are similar to the footprints of a sheep. The toes of the deer, however, are more pointed and are more concave underneath, which affects the shape of the slots and produces a somewhat convex impression on the ground. A deer preparing to leap a fence, landing after a jump or simply skidding on slippery ground puts more of each foot onto the ground than normal and it is sometimes possible to see the impression of the two small toes called dew claws, which do not usually touch the ground, in addition to the prints made by the main two toes. Another clue is the presence of droppings, which in roe deer are pellets of fibrous material, square at one end and pointed at the other.

Even in the absence of slots or droppings, the effect of roe deer upon the trees themselves is usually painfully obvious. They are principally browsing animals and crop the tender tips of the shoots from any trees they can reach. This produces a bushy topiary effect on the side branches of the browsed trees and, if the tree is very young, they will even eat the main growing tip of the leading shoot, thereby causing irremediable damage. If the young trees are able to produce leaders out of reach of roe deer then they stand a chance of being able to grow normally.

In winter, if the weather is severe, with deep snow over a long period, roe deer become so hungry that they are forced to eat the bark of trees. Willows of all kinds are especially prone to being damaged in this way, as are rowans, while conifers and birches seem to escape being eaten. However, removing the bark from a tree is a difficult operation for a deer. For, although deer are herbivorous, they cannot nibble vegetation using their front teeth, as sheep do, because at the front of

Above A male catkin of the goat willow comes into flower in early spring.

Opposite (top) The polecat often occurs in forests, especially where the woodland is fairly open. Nowadays, within the British Isles, they are confined to Wales.

Opposite (bottom) A fine young roe buck with well grown antlers.

Above A young Norway spruce severely browsed by roe deer has at last managed to grow tall enough to escape their reach.

Left The slots of a roe deer.

the mouth there are teeth in the lower jaw only, which means that a deer is unable to bite pieces of bark off a tree. Instead, it has to grip the bark between the incisors of the lower jaw and the hard gum of the upper jaw, then jerk its head upwards. As a result, a length of bark is torn away from the tree in the shape of a long tapering inverted V – an effect referred to as 'stripping'.

Roe deer are highly territorial animals and always live in family groups consisting of two adults, a buck and a doe, and one, or more often two, young. The size of the territory is the area which the buck can hold successfully and this depends upon several factors, such as the age and health of the buck and the amount of cover and food available. In a forest the population will be at its highest where there is an abundant food supply, as in clearings, along rides or at the edge of the forest near to where trees are growing densely together to provide good cover. In such places the size of the territory will be small with a family of roe deer occupying every four or five hectares.

At those times of year when the bucks are sexually most active, during the mating or 'rutting' seasons, the buck defends his territory vigorously and marks both the boundaries of his territory and prominent ground within it. He does this by rubbing the scent glands located on the top of his head against small trees and shrubs, preferring those which are young enough to be springy and avoiding those which are too solid or prickly. As he does so, the bark of the tree is damaged, being scored by the antlers rubbing up and down. Sometimes a complete section of bark is removed and this 'ringing' often kills the tree. The damage done to trees by the bucks is known as 'fraying' and is a major problem for foresters in many areas.

The main rutting season for roe deer, which takes place in June, is marked by increased fraying activity and by frequent boundary disputes, with loud barking matches between bucks and occasional chases

and fights. The bucks also tend to scrape small areas of ground with their feet, producing loose patches of grass and moss, and often chase the does round and round a single tree or round a small group of trees, so that a 'roe ring' is formed on the ground.

There is a second though less intense rutting period in winter. Interestingly, there is a delay in the implantation and development of any embryos resulting from successful summer mating, though this is not so with winter matings. As a result all young, whether conceived the previous summer or winter, are born at the same time, in late May.

Certain other animals and plants, like roe deer, increase their populations when previously open areas of moorland are planted and converted to coniferous forest. Common woodland birds such as woodpigeons and jays find a suitable habitat where they were previously unable to live, as do much less common or widespread species such as the hen harrier and capercaillie.

The population of hen harriers has increased considerably now that more moorland areas are planted with conifers. They are ground-nesting birds and find the thick vegetation in young conifer plantations particularly favourable for nesting sites. They feed principally on small birds and hunt in open moorland for species such as meadow pipits and skylarks. Female hen harriers are fairly inconspicuous, with plumage in shades of brown, apart from the white rump; but the male, though smaller, is much more obvious, being a pale bluish-grey in colour, which makes him easily seen against a sombre moorland background. The hunting bird quarters the ground, flying lazily but strongly – until a potential prey is flushed from cover, when it seizes it immediately. More often than not the harrier will work along a stone wall, dropping first on one side then on the other, occasionally seeming to hang in the air or even slide backwards in the wind as it works along, watching for a small bird to break cover.

Above The capercaillie nests on the ground, usually at the base of a tree.

Below A male hen harrier alights at its nest.

Hen harrier chicks.

In a sense afforestation of open moorland is really reforestation – the replacing of forest on land where the natural forest has been destroyed. Yet a large plantation of Sitka spruce of course bears little resemblance, either floristically or in terms of insects, birds or other animal life, to the native deciduous broadleaved woodland systems originally present. The continuing and sometimes bitter argument concerning the so-called conflict between wildlife and forestry has spawned extreme views on both sides. But, just as it is untrue that large conifer plantations are invariably good for wildlife, it is equally untrue that all planting of conifers is invariably bad for wildlife. The truth lies somewhere in between.

Opposite The blue sowthistle is one of our rare mountain plants specially protected by law.

6 CONSERVATION

What exactly does conservation mean? There are as many definitions as there are people who use the word. The popular usage is near to the idea of 'preservation' and there is no doubt that preserving things is part of the concept of conservation. To many people the two words mean much the same thing, but there is an important difference. The basic concept of preservation is to keep something safe and to protect it from change. This can have a seemingly negative connotation if the fundamental aim is to prevent something happening. Indeed, the protection of rare species may well involve keeping people out of an area, the construction of fences, the erection of notice boards, and in some cases even a twenty-four hour guard. However, this kind of preservation and protection can form part of a comprehensive conservation plan and the whole approach then becomes a more positive one. The conservationist is

concerned with the use of our natural resources, acknowledging that the countryside has to be managed so as to provide all the things we need from it. But, for the conservationist, this has to be achieved in such a way as to maintain and enhance our natural resources without damage or destruction so that we can continue to benefit from them in the long term and pass them on intact to posterity.

The idea of 'natural' resources causes some difficulty. It is often taken to apply to something unaffected by man and hence, erroneously, the conservationist is supposed to be concerned with the 'natural' environment and not with the man-made landscape. This leads to the common belief that conservation only happens in nature reserves and has nothing to do with the ordinary countryside.

If 'natural' means totally unaffected by human activity, then there is very little that is natural left on this planet. Nevertheless, there are different degrees of human impact and some situations are 'more natural' than others. To the conservationist man is seen as part of the system, not as something outside it, and a conservation strategy does not envisage man and nature as opposites.

Whereas the pure preservationist may try to arrest change, the conservationist has to accept that change is the normal way of the world. Species become extinct and new species evolve; there are seasonal cycles and daily cycles. Change is the norm, but our human instincts resist change. We simply do not like to see an animal become extinct or a fine tree fall. It is sometimes hard to accept that change may be an important part of a conservation plan.

The countryside undergoes incessant changes which result from normal management practices and the ecological balance of our environment reflects the impact of such management. Most problems arise when the pace and scale of the changes in management practice are intensified and the ecological balance is violently disturbed. Conservation problems are rapidly becoming more serious and more acute because of the accelerating rate of development of new techniques, technologies, chemical applications and mechanical capabilities.

Threats to the upland environment

The upland environment of Britain is now under threat as never before because we now have the means and the know-how to effect great changes very rapidly in the ways we use upland resources. We are able to change moorland into forests and valleys into reservoirs, to quarry away mountain sides, to 'improve' huge areas of unproductive hillside and to drain the most intractable bog. Indeed, we have the machinery and expertise to change our environment on a scale undreamed of even a generation ago. The worry is whether we are sufficiently aware of our responsibilities to use such power sensibly.

A great deal of our uplands is the product of our past activity. The great tracts of moorland were created from forests and are maintained as moorland by burning and grazing – and are therefore at the less 'natural' end of the spectrum. At the other extreme are tracts of mountainous country, sometimes extending over large areas, particularly in Scotland, where the hand of man has fallen less heavily. There are open areas above the treeline inaccessible except by narrow tracks or on foot where from one year to the next the occasional shepherd or deer stalker is the only human intruder. These are the truly wild places that some would call 'wilderness'. They are progressively being penetrated by more roads, new hill tracks, more sophisticated cross-country vehicles and an increasingly mobile society demanding access for recreation. The wilderness is being eroded and the special quality of such places is becoming more and more difficult to find. This is true not only in Britain but also in Europe and to some extent worldwide.

In the mountains there are still some places almost entirely unaffected by man. The cliffs, screes and wide summit plateaux are as near to 'natural' as any habitats in Britain. There are, of course, exceptions, places where human intrusion has created a massive impact. The summit of Snowdon could hardly be considered unaffected by human activity.

The uplands generally are ecologically fragile. In mountains and moorlands the ecological systems are finely balanced. Often the climate is severe, so growing seasons are short and the production of vegetation is reduced. Plants and animals struggle to exist and to survive and the processes of establishment, growth and succession are terribly slow. Soils are commonly poor, cold, acid and often unstable. They are inhospitable places for wildlife, whose fragile ecosystems develop slowly and are easily destroyed. Once damaged or destroyed, they may recover or regenerate only after long periods of time, if at all.

Sensible use of our upland resources should be based upon a complete understanding of the way they work, the things that live there and the processes that occur. A great deal of effort has gone into research to discover more about upland ecosystems and much is known about them, but the people who have the greatest knowledge of mountains and moorlands are the first to admit how little we really know. Our management of upland resources still retains something of a trial and error element and this is in itself a contributory factor to the threats to our uplands.

A lush field of grass in the lowlands on a good soil in a kind climate will grow fast and provide a lot of good quality food for grazing animals. If, for a while, it becomes overgrazed and the growth rate of the grass is unable to keep pace, it is not a disaster. The farmer gives the field a rest, the grass recovers and grazing, perhaps at a reduced level, can start again. On a mountainside with thin acid soil and a harsh climate there is a much smaller quantity of poorer quality grazing. If there is over-grazing, however slight, the vegetation will be severely damaged. Even if the grazing pressure can be reduced or removed it may be a matter of years before the vegetation recovers. In some places, such as steep slopes with thin soils, the result may be soil erosion leading to complete loss of soil and permanent loss of grazing. The fragility of upland systems and the slowness of the processes at work in them mean that the margin for error is much less than in a lowland situation. Mistakes are easier to make and they have more disastrous and more permanent conse-quences.

The most extensive form of land use in the uplands is farming, normally animal hus-bandry. The impact is mostly at the lower levels of moorland where grazing and, in places, trampling affect the moorland veg-etation. Flocks of sheep play their part in maintaining the treeless nature of moorland and tend to encourage grass moorland at the expense of heather.

Improvement

It is becoming increasingly common for hill farmers to undertake 'improvements' to their hill grazings in order to increase the pro-ductivity of the vegetation and hence its grazing value. Such improvements involve a combination of measures, such as drainage of wet areas, scarification or even ploughing of the surface and reseeding with a grass mixture, coupled with the application of fer-tilisers, depending on the precise site conditions. This is clearly a threat in the very

real sense that it can involve total destruction of the moorland systems. There are some upland areas, for example Exmoor, where the scale of these operations has increased to such an extent that there is now a serious threat to wildlife.

Country sports

Sporting interests such as shooting and deer-stalking overlap a good deal with agricultural and forestry land use. Inasmuch as good grouse moor management requires a regular burning programme, it has a fundamental sig-nificance for conservation. If the objective is to encourage the regeneration and re-establishment of the 'natural' woodland that existed previously, then regular burning is obviously a bad thing. But burning largely created this ecosystem as we know it and if the objective is to conserve the grouse-moor com-munity, maintenance of the burning regime is essential. On the whole those whose interest is in sporting activity are conservationists, if for no other reason than an interest in main-taining their sport. Such conflict as exists is about the subject of vermin. To the old-fashioned gamekeeper 'vermin' was just about any animal or bird which was not 'game'. Certainly any animal with sharp teeth and any bird with a hooked beak were viewed as vermin and were to be eliminated. Today it is generally realised that nature is not as simple as that. There are no goodies or baddies and a more sensitive and enlightened approach to management has developed. That is not to say that poisoned eggs and pole traps are a thing of the past, but legislation and more particu-larly education and public opinion are un-doubtedly changing the attitude of keepers and proprietors. For a bird like the peregrine falcon, whose greatest enemy was once the gamekeeper and more recently pesticide pollution, the biggest threat is now from egg thieves and those who steal the young from the nest to sell to foreign falconers. The keeper's role is now that of protector.

A varied landscape with a great diversity of habitat is rich in wildlife.

Forest conservation

Afforestation has resulted in drastic ecological changes over large areas of uplands during this century and is still continuing to expand, mostly at the expense of hill farming. Projections indicate a potential for further expansion in the next century. Upland forests are virtually entirely coniferous, with their own systems of wildlife, quite different from the open hillsides they clothe. They have a marked impact on the local hydrological conditions, affecting drainage and run-off and hence the characteristics of adjacent systems and whole catchments. They have chemical effects on streams and rivers too, particularly where fertilisers are applied. The establishment of forests in an upland landscape can affect the movement of animals. Where there are extended lengths of fencing to exclude deer from forestry land, for example, care needs to be taken that they are sited so as not to create barriers to the established movements of herds of red deer. In addition there is the emotive issue of the visual impact of large coniferous blocks in open hill country, where great care and skill is needed in designing the planting to harmonise with the landscape. The conversion of open moorland into forests causes dramatic changes in the habitats available to wildlife. Locally there will be total destruction of some existing habitats and losses of associated species – and they will be replaced by different habitats and different species. On a purely local basis this may be regarded as an impoverishment of the wildlife resource. On a broader basis, the increased diversification of habitats by the introduction of forestry to an area and the resulting increase in wildlife constitute an enhancement of the wildlife resource. In a landscape which already has extensive areas of forests, there would be little if any gain for nature conservation from the introduction of more of the same type of woodland. In places where forestry is the dominant existing land use, the remaining open areas may become refuges for some wildlife and any further afforestation may be a real threat to conservation.

Diversity

For effective conservation the ideal land use pattern is a balanced mixture of different uses. A key concept in conservation is diversity, hence the practical conservationist is concerned with the maintenance and enhancement of as great a variety of wildlife as possible. The maximum diversity of species of plants and animals occurs where there is maximum diversity of habitat; and there is the greatest diversity of habitat where, other things being equal, there is the greatest diversity of land use. So, within the upland landscape, where there is a mixture of forestry, open hillside and agricultural land the wildlife resource is richer than in areas where one of these predominates.

This concept holds true on a smaller scale too. Within a forest there are a number of different habitats. Some of these, for example ponds and streams, are natural features with their own special habitats and communities. Others are created as a result of routine forest management. The forest edge, clearings and roadsides, for example, each contribute a slightly different set of conditions for plants and animals to exploit as places to live. Through careful planning, without excessive expense and effort, it is possible to do a great deal in forests to create new habitats in the interests of nature conservation without detriment to commercial forest management. The key is to create as much variety in the environment as possible and to break up large areas of uniform monoculture.

Recreation and tourism

The increasing mobility of a comparatively affluent, leisured and car-owning society with a modern road network at its disposal has, with other factors, created a new threat to upland conservation. Large numbers of people now find it possible to travel to parts of the country which not so many years ago were difficult to get to. The moors of the Peak District are within easy reach of literally millions of people and all our other upland areas are easily accessible from one large conurbation or another, enabling many of us to spend a holiday, a weekend, or even just a few hours among the hills of Wales, the Lake District or Scotland.

For many people an upland outing or holiday is inspired simply by a desire to escape, however briefly, from the rush and noise of the city to the peace and quiet of the hills, for a chance to be alone, to enjoy the fresh air and to relax. In a fairly passive way they enjoy the views of mountains, cliffs, rocks and waterfalls, and appreciate the open country and the colours and dramatic character of the landscape. Mostly they focus on tourist centres where there are facilities to cater for them and, if the coach should stop in the open country, at a well-known viewpoint perhaps, they do not venture far from the vehicle or for long. In the immediate vicinity of a lay-by, picnic site or car park there is in-

evitably an impact on the surrounding vegetation both from people and cars, as vehicles are driven over it and people walk or picnic on it. The fact that tourists rarely move far from their cars ensures that damage is confined to a fairly small area.

For others, recreation in the hills is a more active affair and, as a result, their potential impact on the countryside is that much greater. Many people derive great pleasure from rambling and hillwalking. There is physical challenge in a long-distance walk or the struggle to the top of a hill. A lot of people follow long-distance footpaths, such as the Pennine Way, or go 'Munro-bagging', which entails conquering all the mountains in Britain over 3,000 feet high. Whatever their motive – whether physical, or an interest in natural history or the countryside, or indeed spiritual satisfaction – their very presence may be damaging, since the wear and tear caused by hundreds of pairs of feet can create serious erosion. Some kinds of terrain are able to withstand severe trampling better than others. The carrying capacity of dry grassland on the level is far greater than that of wet, peaty soils on steep slopes, where permanent damage can be caused even by low levels of visitors and tourists. There are formidable management problems in coping with a

Birds such as lapwing (left) and curlew (right) often desert their eggs if disturbed by hill walkers and their dogs. In some areas lapwing are also being affected by loss of habitat.

Opposite Scots pines severely damaged by red deer.

Above A new track winds into the hills, impossible to disguise.

situation, as on parts of the Pennine Way, where large numbers of people follow more or less the same route across sensitive ground such as exposed blanket peat. A whole new technology, with new techniques and materials, has evolved to provide solutions to this kind of problem – but the environmental damage is there and the threat to conservation grows yearly.

Wherever there is a car park with a recognised route to a nearby beauty spot or hilltop, a footpath is created by the passage of many feet. In mountain country this makes a scar on the hillside where damaged vegetation has led to erosion. Also a water track may be formed, soil lost and stony ground laid bare. The result is a line visible for miles around.

Earth-moving machinery

Even more obvious are the gashes on hillsides created by the building of rough tracks to take cross-country vehicles further into the hills. This is another threat to the delicate upland ecosystems resulting from the proliferation of powerful and versatile machinery, in this case heavy digging and earth-moving equipment. Every year more and more tracks are built to enable the shepherds, keepers and others who work on the moors and in the hills to do their jobs more easily and more effectively.

Winter sports

The demands made on the countryside by the burgeoning recreation industry range in intensity from the relatively simple requirements of the rock climber, who only needs access and a rock face, to the sophisticated paraphernalia of a winter sports development, with its ski-lifts, pistes and restaurants at the other extreme. The rock climber, especially if exploring new faces and establishing new routes, can have a local impact in places where there are patches of vegetation on the cliff, by scraping the plants off and cleaning up the ledges. But this is as nothing compared with the environmental impact of a skiing development.

Limited as winter sports may be in Britain at the present time, their popularity has grown over recent years and there is sustained pressure to extend existing facilities and develop new areas. Inevitably, suitable sites for skiing are upland sites with steep slopes and gullies which will hold snow – sites that are highly susceptible to damage. Even large numbers of skiers on good snow cover may do little environmental harm beyond creating a local centre of disturbance, though there is some evidence to suggest that compacting of snow on ski runs affects the community underneath. But fewer people skiing on inadequate snow cover can do serious damage.

There is much concern about some skiing developments on amenity grounds. The visual impact of hill paths and tracks pales into insignificance alongside the jumble of ski-tows, chairlifts, tracks, ditches, fences, car parks, buildings, coils of old wire and oil drums which, in summer particularly, give an impression of a sprawling building site. Not even by the wildest stretch of the imagination could these be thought attractive or an enhancement of the beauty of the landscape. However, the threat to conservation is not the skiing itself, nor the messiness of the development, but the damage to the extremely sensitive ecosystem caused during construction and maintenance work. The building of a chairlift or ski-tow involves the delivery of fairly large, heavy structures, cables, concrete and the like to the site for installation. There is then ongoing maintenance, which demands regular visits and inspections.

Nowadays helicopters are used increasingly for this work, and much environmental damage can be avoided. In the past, however, tracked vehicles were invariably used to carry materials up the mountainside. The effect on the vegetation of a tracked vehicle climbing a slope is disastrous. The surface of the ground is broken, the vegetation damaged and in a short time there is serious erosion. On repeated journeys up the hill the line of the original route becomes churned up to such an extent as to become unusable, so the vehicle takes a slightly different route and the area of devastation spreads wider and wider.

In the initial stages woody shrubs such as heather are destroyed, the plants able to survive longest being those with an underground rhizome system, such as cloudberry. But a macerated bed of loose peat and sand on a steep slope is in no way stable and the first heavy rain storm will flush the whole lot down the hill. Where an access track has been built there is further danger and the excavation of the ditches under ski-tows, needed to encourage the necessary track of snow, is a perfect recipe for erosion.

Chairlifts, unlike tows, can operate in summer without snow and offer a quick and easy way for large numbers of people to be taken up a mountain. This may be a good thing, but it does create litter and damage by hundreds of trampling feet – maybe close to sensitive areas of unique wildlife significance.

The needs of society

Some threats to upland conservation arise from the needs of society as a whole rather than the activities of individuals. A growing population exerts increasing pressure on finite

Above Erosion caused by a skiing development.

Below Modern communications demand a modern road network. The trunk road to Inverness passes through the Highlands.

resources.

Demand for greater and more reliable supplies of water in towns and cities and for industry means that more and more valleys are flooded to create reservoirs. The need for cheaper and more plentiful electricity from clean, renewable and non-polluting sources means that more and more hydroelectric schemes are built, so more dams are constructed and more valleys flooded.

Large tracts of upland country, closed to most other users, are used for military training, perhaps because upland areas are cheaper and more suitable than lowland ones for such a purpose. Paradoxically, in areas used for military training, where the authorities are alert to the needs of conservation and other threats are absent, wildlife is safer than almost anywhere else.

Power lines, roads, oil and gas pipe-lines all pass through moorland and mountainous countryside; and because of the open nature of the landscape and its sensitive ecological character, careful design and construction are if anything more important than in the lowlands.

Conservation organisations

Many individuals and organisations care about what happens to our environment and many bodies are concerned in one way or another with conservation. Some of these are statutory bodies financed from the public purse. Principal among these is the Nature Conservancy Council, whose prime concern is nature conservation in general, but several other statutory bodies are responsible for specific aspects

The hard, bare shore-line of a hydroelectric reservoir results from the unnatural fluctuations in water level.

of conservation, such as the Countryside Commission, the Countryside Commission for Scotland and the Forestry Commission. These public bodies have particular responsibilities laid upon them, as have local authorities, and they have powers to take action with regard to conservation.

In addition to the statutory bodies there are a host of voluntary organisations (among them the British Naturalists' Association) which anyone can join and which in varying degrees consider nature conservation to be their concern. The naturalists' trusts are the foremost voluntary organisations whose prime concern is nature conservation. But local natural history and scientific societies and specialist national groups are all involved

in conservation work to some extent, too. Some of these, such as the Royal Society for the Protection of Birds, the National Trust and the National Trust for Scotland, are very large organisations. Others, like the British Bryological Society, only have a small membership.

Nature reserves

One of the many ways in which these bodies seek to conserve our wildlife resources is the establishment of reserves. Originally preservationist in concept, many of them are still real sanctuaries for wildlife, but most are also more than that and provide opportunities for research and education. A reserve is managed according to an agreed plan depending on its particular objectives. The Nature Conservancy Council can declare National Nature Reserves, which are important areas for

The shore of Loch Lubnaig, an area under the care of the Forestry Commission.

Above The otter, which sometimes inhabits upland sites, is now a protected species.

Left Red-throated diver – tiny upland lochs need to be conserved if this rare species is to continue breeding in Britain.

nature conservation in the national or even international context, but many voluntary bodies also establish reserves according to their own criteria. Altogether there are a large number of reserves that include moorland and mountainous countryside.

The Nature Conservancy Council also has a duty to designate Sites of Special Scientific Interest. There are many more of these than there are reserves and again many of them are examples of upland ecosystems.

Active conservation in reserves is only a small part of the broad nature conservation effort and all these bodies do many other things as well. Publications, meetings, advice,

Beinn Eighe National Nature Reserve in Wester Ross in an area of international conservation importance

surveys and education are all used as ways of achieving the conservation goal.

Actually achieving this objective is, of course, the difficult part. The fate of our countryside is the result of many complex pressures and the landscape which we create is the result of all these influences put together over a period of time. In addition to the ecological constraints imposed by the location, the rocks and the climate, the reasons for the existence of one particular landscape pattern rather than another can be economic, social, political or personal. Generally, a landowner will use his land in the way which makes most economic and commercial sense, but one particular form of land use can deliberately be made more or less profitable than another by manipulation of economic factors such as taxation or government grants. If a political decision is taken that forestry should be encouraged or discouraged, either end can be achieved by altering the arrangements for taxation of woodlands and conditions for grant aid for planting. At the end of the day each individual will make his own decision to suit his own circumstances and land use on the two sides of a boundary fence may be quite different.

The future

To achieve the conservation ideal requires that these complex pressures should work towards the particular goal of nature conservation. The main weapons in this attempt are planning, education and common sense.

It offends against common sense to have a situation where one government agency offers a landowner a grant to drain a piece of land while another government agency offers him compensation not to, or where the owner of a hill loch faces a penalty under one Act of Parliament if he interferes with the water level

Inverpolly National Nature Reserve.

The climate and soils are the same, the ownership is different.

and a penalty under another if he doesn't.

Plans drawn up on a national, regional or local scale can help to define land use objectives and to allocate priorities in general or in particular cases. Extensive surveys are required to provide the data on which such plans are based and these can be valuable in themselves as part of the basic inventory of our wildlife resources. Unfortunately, not all plans are as well formulated nor all surveys as comprehensively conducted as one might wish.

Local planning authorities are responsible for the control of development in their own areas and by the use of planning controls they are able to exert a great influence on nature conservation. They can, for instance, control building operations, recreational developments, caravan sites, quarrying and so on, but major land uses such as agriculture and forestry enterprises are not subject to planning control. Of course, development control has little effect if it is not used or effectively enforced, and enforcement is not always easy.

Planning is a matter for public concern. The policies of local authorities and planning decisions derive in the last analysis from public opinion and there are conservationists who argue that the proper use of our resources depends on the public being sufficiently well informed. They maintain that a vocal, well informed public will ensure, through the democratic processes, that a wise and sensible conservation path is followed and that we shall in future avoid the perpetration of the sort of acts of environmental vandalism that have occurred all too often in the past. The key to achieving this well informed body of public opinion is education in the broadest sense.

People cannot care about something if they know nothing about it and conservation entails informing the public, through all possible means – books, radio, television, films, newspapers, public meetings and interpretation of the countryside on site. If people are informed about the countryside and its wildlife, and understand something of how it works, they are more likely to care about what happens to it.

Some conservationists believe that in the long run education is the only way of achieving lasting nature conservation. Others fear it is already too late. What is certain is that it is vitally important for the future of our upland heritage that all of us do whatever we can – both for its own sake and for posterity.

FURTHER READING

Ball, D. F., Dale, J., Sheail, J. and Heal, O. W., *Vegetation Change in Upland Landscape* (Institute of Terrestrial Ecology, 1982).

Bridges, E. M., *World Soils* (Cambridge University Press, 1970).

Condry, W. M., *The Snowdonia National Park* (Collins, 1966).

Darling, F. F. and Boyd, J. M., *The Highlands and Islands* (Collins, 1947).

Department of Agriculture and Fisheries for Scotland and Nature Conservancy Council, *A Guide to Good Muirburn Practice* (HMSO, 1977).

Edwards, K. C., *The Peak District* (Collins, 1962).

Forestry Commission, *Forestry Practice* (HMSO, 1978).

Forestry Commission, *Forestry in the Landscape* (HMSO, 1966).

Forestry Commission, *Wildlife Conservation in Woodlands* (HMSO, 1972).

Gimmingham, C. H., *An Introduction to Heathland Ecology* (Oliver & Boyd, 1975).

Gimmingham, C. H., *Ecology of Heathlands* (Chapman & Hall, 1972).

Godwin, Sir H., *The Archives of the Peat Bogs* (Cambridge University Press, 1981).

Gordon, S. P., *The Golden Eagle* (Collins, 1955).

Harvey, L. A. and St Leger-Gordon, D., *Dartmoor* (Collins, 1963).

Kirkaldy, J. F., *Minerals and Rocks* (Blandford, 1963).

Leutscher, A., *The Ecology of Mountains* (Franklin Watts, 1978).

Miles, J., *Effect of Birch on Moorlands* (Institute of Terrestrial Ecology, 1981).

Miles, P. M. and Miles, H. B., *Chalkland and Moorland Ecology* (Hulton, 1968).

Moore, P. D. and Bellamy, D. J., *Peatlands* (Elek, 1974).

Nature Conservancy Council, *Plant Communities of the Scottish Highlands* (HMSO, 1962).

Nethersole-Thompson, D. and M., *Greenshanks* (Poyser, 1979).

North, F. J., Cambell, B. and Scott, R., *Snowdonia* (Collins, 1949).

Pearsall, W. H., *Mountains and Moorlands* (Collins, 1950).

Pearsall, W. H. and Pennington, W., *The Lake District* (Collins, 1973).

Ratcliffe, D., *The Peregrine Falcon* (Poyser, 1980).

Raven, J. and Walters, S. M., *Mountain Flowers* (Collins, 1956).

Stamp, L. D., *Britain's Structure and Scenery* (Collins, 1946).

Sparks, B. W. and West, R. G., *The Ice Age in Britain* (Methuen, 1972).

Watson, D., *The Hen Harrier* (Poyser, 1977).

West, R. G., *Studying the Past by Pollen Analysis* (Oxford University Press, 1971).

Weyman, D. and V., *Landscape Processes* (Allen & Unwin), 1977.

ACKNOWLEDGEMENTS

I am deeply grateful to Carole Pugh for her splendid line drawings; to Ron Freethy for his enthusiastic encouragement; to my wife Margaret for her meticulous proofreading; to the several photographers mentioned below for permission to use their many excellent photographs; to Peter Leek of The Crowood Press for his patience; and, not least, to the many people in whose company over the years I have come to know and love the hills.

PICTURE CREDITS

Colour and Black & White Photos

John Barron: *pages* 67 (top), 93
Brian Brookes: frontispiece, *pages* 10–11, 14 (both), 17, 18, 19 (bottom), 22, 32, 34 (both), 35 (bottom), 42–3, 46–7, 50 (both), 51, 52, 54, 57 (bottom), 58 (both), 70 (both), 71, 73, 74, 75 (both), 77 (right), 78 (both), 82, 86, 90 (top), 91, 94–5, 99 (all), 103, 106–7, 110, 111, 113 (both), 114–15, 122
Barry Candy: *page* 57 (top)
Michael Clark: *pages* 27 (top), 98 (both)
Elizabeth Davenport: *page* 15
Gordon Dickson: *page* 90 (bottom)
J. H. Dickson: *page* 41 (all)
Michael Edwards: *pages* 25, 29,

30, 31, 59 (both), 76, 85, 102, 109 (right), 117 (bottom), 118–19, 120–1
Forestry Commission, Edinburgh: *pages* 87, 89, 116
Ron Freethy: *pages* 26 (top), 27 (bottom), 117 (top)
E. C. M. Haes: *pages* 13, 19 (top), 20
Alan W. Heath: *pages* 38 (top and bottom left), 48, 55, 77 (left), 97
Margaret Hodge: *page* 39 (both)
Eric and David Hosking: *pages* 23, 63 (bottom), 64, 67 (bottom), 80 (top), 101 (top)
T. J. James: *page* 62
Charles Linford: *pages* 26 (bottom), 80 (bottom), 81

W. S. Pitt: *page* 101 (bottom)
Chris Rowley: *page* 35 (top)
Ian Spellerberg: *page* 38 (bottom right)
Bill Wilkinson: *pages* 61, 63 (top), 109 (left)

Cover Photos

Top left: Bernard Lee
Top right: Brian Brookes
Bottom left: Brian Brookes
Bottom right: Michael Edwards

Line Drawings

The line illustrations are by Carole Pugh.

INDEX